S0-CMZ-937

STUDIES IN QUALITATIVE METHODOLOGY

Volume 5 • 1995

COMPUTING AND QUALITATIVE RESEARCH

STUDIES IN QUALITATIVE METHODOLOGY

COMPUTING AND QUALITATIVE RESEARCH

Editor: ROBERT G. BURGESS
Department of Sociology and
Centre for Educational Development, Appraisal and Research (CEDAR)
University of Warwick

VOLUME 5 • 1995

Greenwich, Connecticut *London, England*

55 Old Post Road No. 2
Greenwich, Connecticut 06836

JAI PRESS LTD.
The Courtyard
28 High Street
Hampton Hill
Middlesex TW12 1PD
England

ISBN: 1-55938-902-8

Manufactured in the United States of America

CONTENTS

PREFACE

Each volume of *Studies in Qualitative Methodology*publishes papers that follow similar themes relating to qualitative research. Earlier volumes have focused on the conduct of qualitative research (Volume 1), research experience (Volume 2), the learning experience for a group of researchers who have conducted their first major study at doctoral level (Volume 3), and further first-hand accounts together with commentaries on major issues concerned with qualitative research and qualitative researchers (Volume 4). This volume continues with some of these themes: personal accounts and lessons that can be learned from actual projects. The focus of this collection is upon the use of computers in qualitative research.

In common with other volumes in this annual review series, there is a brief introduction to contextualize the papers that follow. However, in common with many annual review publications and journals, editorial commentary has been confined to the introduction rather than through a lengthy essay review within the volume.

Those readers who wish to obtain further details about this series of volumes, or who have material for consideration, should contact me at the Department of Sociology/CEDAR, University of Warwick, Coventry, CV4 7AL, England.

Robert Burgess
Editor

INTRODUCTION

There are now numerous texts, collections of readings, and empirical studies that focus on qualitative research. Many of these volumes put the emphasis on the collection of qualitative data with the result that there has been a range of work which focuses on methods of data collection. Indeed, even sets of essays that focus on the process of doing research seem to spend more time on the data collection phase of social investigation.

It is only in recent years that researchers have turned their attention to other aspects of the research process including sponsorship and research design (Burgess 1993), data analysis in qualitative work (Bryman and Burgess 1994), dissemination and writing (Atkinson 1990), and the evaluation of qualitative studies (Hammersley 1992). The result has been a shift toward some of the ways in which different phases of the research process interact with each other.

In concentrating on data analysis, writers have not only been concerned with the use of data, but also with the approach that is taken to analyze qualitative data. While 20 years ago many researchers would have focused upon the use of field notes to combine and recombine in terms of themes, many contemporary qualitative researchers have started to explore the potential of new technology in general, and micro computers and software in particular (Fielding and Lee 1991). Much of the interest in this area has focused on an assessment of software which, although very useful, does not take us toward a critical evaluation of the way in which technology can be used in actual projects as opposed to set piece demonstrations.

The papers that are brought together in this volume follow in the tradition of essays in earlier volumes of *Studies in Qualitative Methodology* by focusing on research practice. In this respect, the researchers' evaluations of software for qualitative data analysis takes place in the context of *actual* projects. The papers, therefore, provide a discussion of several themes, including:

(A) the context of computer use in qualitative research;
(B) the presentation and potential of a range of software packages;
(C) the experience of using a computer to analyze qualitative data; and
(D) an evaluation of the advantages, disadvantages, and further areas where development is required on the use of computers in qualitative research.

Each paper takes up some of these themes in the context of researchers' experiences of doing qualitative research and using software to analyze data.

OVERVIEW

The papers in this volume draw on the experience of researchers who have used computers when conducting qualitative research in a variety of circumstances on a range of projects that included small scale doctoral studies and team-based multi-site case studies. In each paper, an assessment is provided of the software used and the way it was handled alongside other approaches. However, some of the earlier papers in the volume set the debate about computer use in qualitative research in context.

We begin with a paper by Nigel G. Fielding and Raymond M. Lee who examine somc of the difficulties that researchers face when attempting to choose Computer Assisted Qualitative Data Analysis Software (CAQDAS). They highlight the issues that need to be considered in choosing software that is appropriate to the researchers' analytic requirements. The authors also examine the role of programs in social research and their effect on research teams. Finally, they look at some of the implications for research training. It is some of these themes that are taken up in subsequent papers.

In the second paper, Sharlene Hesse-Biber takes up some of the controversies that surround the use of computers in qualitative data analysis. Among the concerns she examines are fears that computer technology will separate the researcher from the creative process; that computer programs will superimpose the logic of survey research on qualitative data; that the computer will dictate the analysis; that qualitative measures associated with reliability and validity will be used; and that issues of confidentiality will be more acute when software is used. To address these issues, Sharlene Hesse-Biber draws on her experience of developing and using a software package called HyperRESEARCH™, which she argues assists the researcher by reducing the time required for analysis, introduces labor-saving approaches, and increases the potential for generating and testing theory.

In the third paper, Wilma Mangabeira sketches the historical background and main trends in using computers to analyze social science data before turning to the possibilities of the ethnograph. This program was used to analyze data collected in a study of a steelworks in Brazil. She examines the use of computer assisted analysis of qualitative data compared with the traditional manual approach. Finally, she assesses the implications of this development for sociological paradigms and for research practice. The fourth paper contains a further discussion of the ethnograph by Derrick Armstrong who makes an assessment of its use on the first major project he conducted on the assessment of children's special educational needs. Here, he demonstrates how there is no standard procedure for using the ethnograph. Indeed, he illustrates how the difficulties he encountered resulted in delimiting the use of the software in his project. Similarly, the fifth paper by Annemarie Sprokkereef, Emma Lakin, Christopher J. Pole, and myself, illustrates how the ethnograph was used by our team in conducting a study of postgraduate education and training in the natural sciences and engineering. In common with other researchers, this paper highlights how the software was actually used compared with the way it is claimed it should be used.

In the paper that follows, Lyn Richards introduces the use of NUD•IST (Non-Numerical Unstructured Datas Indexing Searching and Theorising)—a software package that has been developed by Lyn and Tom Richards and widely used by qualitative researchers worldwide. In this paper, she reports on a project concerned with the social construction of the menopause whose design was influenced by the availability of qualitative computing facilities. The researcher focuses on the research design phase of the project and discusses the management of documents, indexing, the use of an index, and the development of links between qualitative and quantitative data.

In the final two papers, a number of the themes raised in earlier papers with respect to individual programs are brought up in relation to a range of software packages as Anna Weaver and Paul Atkinson evaluate The Ethnograph and GUIDE, while Liz Stanley and Bogusia Temple examine askSam, Info Select, The Ethnograph, NUD•IST, Ethno, and the facilities available through Word for Windows.

All together these papers highlight some of the key considerations that need to be taken into account by qualitative researchers when selecting software packages for use on qualitative projects. In turn, the experiences of researchers on these projects will, it is hoped, advance our understanding and use of computers in qualitative data analysis.

REFERENCES

Atkinson, P.
1990 *The Ethnographic Imagination*. London: Routledge.

Bryman, A., and Burgess, R.G. (Eds).
1994 *Analysing Qualitative Data.* London: Routledge.
Burgess, R.G. (Ed).
1993 *Educational Research and Evaluation: For Policy and Practice.* Lewes: Falmer Press.
Fielding, N., and Lee, R. (Eds).
1991 *Using Computers in Qualitative Research.* London: Sage.
Hammersley, M.
1992 *What's Wrong With Ethnography?* London: Routledge.

Robert Burgess
Editor

CONFRONTING CAQDAS:
CHOICE AND CONTINGENCY

Nigel G. Fielding and Raymond M. Lee

Qualitative data, such as interviews, field notes, and extracts from documents, are used in pure and applied research in a number of social science disciplines. Because, by definition, such data cannot easily be quantified, they present practical, technical, and methodological problems when the time comes to analyze the data. In recent years, specialist software has appeared to facilitate the analysis of qualitative data. Awareness and use of this software (hereafter "CAQDAS" or Computer-Assisted Qualitative Data Analysis Software) is rapidly spreading, particularly in applied research in fields like health and market research. While hard data on users is scarce, we have noticed that the majority of participants in our research on CAQDAS users, and those who contact us for advice on choosing software, work in applied research settings. Inspection of lists of registered users of particular programs kept

Studies in Qualitative Methodology, Volume 5, pages 1-23.

ISBN: 1-55938-902-8.

by developers and vendors also suggests that users tend to be associated with research institutes and projects rather than discipline-based academic departments.[1] Perhaps the most systematic information is still that relating to the most commonly used package, The Ethnograph. Of the 115 users who had, by 1990, signed up for networking, the largest group (33) were in education research, followed by nursing research (27), sociologists (17), anthropologists (13), other health disciplines such as occupational therapy (11) and psychologists (9), and individuals from other fields including criminology and political science. Drawing again on our own experiences, we have noticed that another group of intended users are graduate students. In an earlier discussion (Lee and Fielding 1991), we suggested that these concentrations of use indicated that CAQDAS use had been highly instrumental, a response to problems encountered in handling qualitative data on projects bound by one or two-year contracts or the need to prepare a dissertation during the course of graduate study.

To date, little attempt has been made to study the experiences of users of the software, and so there is no systematic information available to researchers wanting to choose the most appropriate software for their particular application, level of computer expertise, and research timetable. In this paper we concern ourselves with a number of factors which we feel need to be taken into account in making informed choices from the range of CAQDAS packages that are currently available. We draw on our experience advising inquirers, a role pressed upon us following the publication of *Using Computers in Qualitative Research*, one of the first books on the subject, which we edited, and as trainers and teachers of research methods and information technology. More particularly, we draw on preliminary findings from qualitative fieldwork which we have conducted on users' experiences of CAQDAS. Our research in this area is based on focus group methodology rather than interviews with individual users. This is because we have sometimes, although not always, found individual users surprisingly unclear about precisely how they use a program. In our experience the sharing of experiences in a group context promotes fruitful discussion of the kinds of issues we are to be concerned with in this paper. Focus groups with past or present CAQDAS users took place during 1992 and 1993. The groups were convened at various sites throughout Great Britain and included users of a wide range of currently available programs. The group discussions covered a range of topics including: how users heard about the program and from whom, what use they had made of it, the nature of their research, the character of their research team if any, how they had analyzed their data using the program and their reactions, both positive and negative, to the software, its availability, documentation, and support. Groups lasted between 90 and 150 minutes and were tape-recorded and transcribed verbatim, with transcripts fed back to participants on request.

In what follows, we briefly review the historical development of social science data analysis software, focusing in particular on the recent emergence of CAQDAS programs. We then sketch in some of the decision points which flow from the acquisition and use of such software as well as some of the choices users make in relation to particular software packages.

Figure 1 shows a time line which displays the development of data analysis software in the social sciences. The dates given are approximate and the distinctions made between different program types are in places somewhat arbitrary. Nevertheless, some clear patterns emerge. First of all, data analysis software in the social sciences has been oriented traditionally toward the needs of quantitative researchers. As Brent and Anderson (1990) show, small-scale, limited programs for performing statistical analyses began to emerge in the mid-1960s. Before long these began to be collected into integrated statistical libraries which could be operated in batch mode on a mainframe computer using a simplified command language. By the mid-1970s, statistical packages of this kind began to be used interactively on mainframe computers and were soon followed by programs capable of providing at least a limited range of statistical procedures on desktop computers. A decade later, fully featured statistical packages had found their way onto microcomputers.

As the time line shows, the use of computer software to analyze non-numeric data is not entirely new. Researchers in the

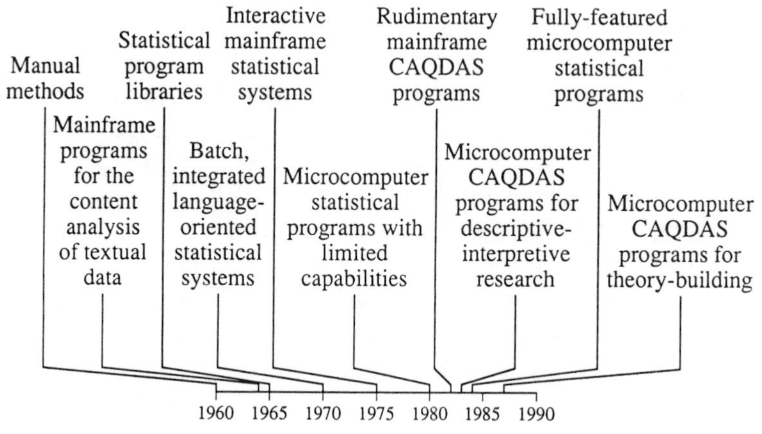

Figure 1. Historical Development of Data Analysis Software in the Social Sciences

humanities, especially those having to deal with very large volumes of textual material, soon became interested in using computers for analyzing textual data (Lee and Fielding 1991). Busa (1980) records, for example, that his first attempt in the period immediately after the Second World War to produce a systematic linguistically-based analysis of the concept of "presence" in the writings of Thomas Acquinas produced 10,000 index cards each containing a single sentence. Soon after he began to recognize that if he were to realize his dream of producing the *Index Thomisticus*, a concordance of all of the writing of Acquinas, he would have to process in excess of 10 million words, an undertaking impossible by manual means but feasible using the computer technology then beginning to emerge. (For this early period in humanities computing, see also Choueka 1980; Morton 1980).

Mainframe-based programs for analyzing text such as OCP (the Oxford Concordance Program), TACT, or BYU Concordance, became widely used in the humanities. Their particular forte is their ability when dealing with large bodies of text to generate breakdowns, say, of the frequency with which particular words or combinations of words are used, to produce "key-words-in-context" lists and concordances.[2] A difficulty with using these programs in qualitative research is that in many of the literary applications for which such programs are most useful, one can quite naturally specify a fixed amount of context, a line say or a sentence, for index or concordance terms. In many social science applications, however, this would be too constraining. The context of an utterance can be a word, a few lines, or several paragraphs. Qualitative researchers, in other words, typically want to define variable-length contexts.

Qualitative researchers who needed to analyze field notes or interview transcripts continued to rely on manual methods, perhaps using colored pens or making multiple copies of relevant segments of field material. Computer packages which aimed to replace these cumbersome and tedious procedures have emerged only recently. First to appear were rudimentary mainframe CAQDAS programs, such as the original versions of The Ethnograph and the now defunct program TAP. However, with some exceptions, subsequent developments have been firmly focused on desktop machines, with a substantial number of programs now being available for IBM PCs and a further sprinkling for the Macintosh platform.

Tesch (1991) distinguishes between CAQDAS programs for descriptive-interpretive research and those which explicitly support theory building. The former assist researchers to delineate and collate patterns or themes appearing in the data. Although, they provide additional features which go beyond manual methods such as the ability to count code frequencies or attach memos to text, such programs mimic by and large traditional "cut and paste" methods. By theory building programs Tesch means programs which aid in the development of sophisticated, interrelated category systems and in some cases hypothesis testing. Although, again there are clear exceptions (one of the earliest programs, NUD•IST, has always firmly embraced theory-building), programs for descriptive-interpretive analysis tended to emerge earlier and still remain more common than their theory-building cousins.

Unlike, for example, statistical packages like SPSS-X, few CAQDAS programs have yet been subject to the full rigors of marketing and post-sales support. Statistical packages are widely used in the academic world across a range of disciplines and are routinely taught to undergraduate students in the social sciences. In addition, statistical software is widely used in business environments. This means that a substantial market exists and funding for future software development is readily available. By contrast, the development of software for qualitative data analysis is not "big business." The market for qualitative analysis software is much smaller than for statistical packages. Users are probably more diffuse in terms of their understanding of what constitutes qualitative analysis than are quantitative researchers. One consequence of the breadth of approaches to qualitative analysis is a proliferation of programs suited to particular analytic approaches, with no one package having all the features necessary to satisfy all qualitative researchers. Another consequence strays into the realm of the epistemological and is best discussed by reference to a particular package, The Ethnograph. This package is associated with the approach to analytic coding associated with grounded theory (Glaser and Strauss 1967), and sometimes colloquially known as "cut and paste" technique. Because John Seidel, the package's developer, wished to retain the emphasis on careful, precise coding which is integral to the grounded theory approach, the first few versions of the package required the researcher to assign codes, manually, off-screen. Seidel wanted to ensure that researchers still paid full attention to coding and categorization; he literally did *not* want to make it "too easy" (personal communication).

We can take this point further by reference to the same package. As noted, The Ethnograph was developed in accord with the methodology and analytic processes associated with grounded theory, an approach itself often associated with the concerns of interactionist sociology. Consequently, researchers attempting to use the package for qualitative work within a different analytic tradition encountered problems. For example, the "code-mapping" process in The Ethnograph suggests a process of classification which is ultimately boiled down to a set of codes attached to lines. Such a procedure can produce a fast-growing and heterogeneous collection of codes which can be hard to relate to each other (the problem has been dealt with in the version under development at the time of writing of this paper by the inclusion of a feature enabling users to write analytical memos recording the reasons for code assignment, as in grounded theory). However, problems remain for conversation analysts and others interested in sequentiality in talk. By providing the opportunity to code and later isolate fragments of text, "cut-and-paste" programs do not provide for an analysis of sequential structures. Rather they invite the consideration of single utterances or larger episodes in isolation. Essentially this reflects the analytic disposition of the program designer. The non-sequential view of, for instance, interview data, is consistent with grounded theory analytic approaches. One very basic problem is that of line length. The Ethnograph takes lines as its basic analytic unit, but this seldom accords with the length of the fragments a conversation analyst will regard as discrete analytic entities. The grounded theory approach is, of course, a widespread one, but it does not suit all users; the more "micro" one's focus the less satisfactory it may be.

Inevitably there is also the opposite problem to that of the "micro" analyst. Agar (1991) is among those who have argued that The Ethnograph and other programs like it are chiefly useful for cutting data up into smaller "chunks" and analyzing these, but less satisfactory for trying to grasp data sets as a whole. In fact, Seidel agrees. He believes that the analysis of discrete chunks is one way to learn something about the data but not the only way (Seidel 1991). Seidel argues that The Ethnograph can facilitate more holistic analysis by making it easier to work back and forth between decontextualized segments and the original context in which these occurred (a program feature means that the immediate context is always displayed immediately after the selected segment in either the single or multiple search procedure). The link between segment and context is the file name and line numbers printed out with every segment. After the user has extracted and analyzed discrete segments a return to the original context may well reveal other things going on which are not represented in the coding scheme and which could not be grasped by simply examining coded segments.

In his article, Seidel gives an example from one of his studies of interaction between nurses and women during the second stage of labor. One of the things a holistic analysis needs to do is to relate parts to the whole. In the labor example, Seidel's team had a code word called "mockup" to identify parts of the transcript where the nurse describes or explains something that has just happened, is currently happening, or will happen in the future. One analytic task was to search for all of the mockups and determine how they were alike and how they differed. Not only could they have different temporal orientations but they could also be about different substantive concerns. Further, they could be generated spontaneously by the nurse or as a response to an inquiry by the woman in labor. Seidel and his colleagues randomly selected a mockup segment and examined it in its original context to get a sense of why that mockup occurred when it did and what else was going on when that mockup was generated. In one case the mockup turned out to be a way of resolving a dispute between the nurse and the woman which had gone on for several hundred lines of transcript. This led them to a new analytic category of nurse/woman disputes, which was not previously represented in their coding scheme and which could not readily be deduced from examining discrete segments. The researchers also gained a better understanding of mockups and their role in the larger flow of interaction.

As this example suggests, CAQDAS software has fewer obvious applications outside the academic world than do statistical packages. Indeed, most qualitative analysis packages have emerged from an academic environment, often produced by qualitative analysts who either themselves possessed the necessary programming skills or had ready access to sympathetic collaborators who provided appropriate technical support. While this has certain advantages to the user in terms of keeping software low in price and responsive to the perceived needs of users, it also has a downside. Information about the availability of software, about potential uses, and the problems involved in using a package is often sparse.

There are signs that information about CAQDAS programs is being introduced into postgraduate training programs. Clearly, too, events such as the Surrey conference in 1989 or one of a number of small-scale workshops or seminars on the topic held subsequently have been useful in alerting qualitative researchers to the possibility of software use.[3] We would hazard a guess that a majority of users hear about software via informal networks. One person we interviewed, for example, heard about The Ethnograph while standing over the departmental photocopier talking with a colleague about the problems of handling large amounts of qualitative data. While informal networks clearly play an important role in diffusing information (Granovetter 1973), they can be haphazard and in some cases inefficient. A crucial problem here is that user networks are often patchy and fragmented in character. We, and others, have experienced this problem in the form of repeated requests for information. These requests can also be commonly found on computer bulletin boards, like Qual-RS, used by qualitative researchers.[4] One further example might bring this point home. In the course of our research we have frequently found that we bring together in a focus group researchers, often working only short geographical distances apart, who had previously not known of the existence of other participants and who were often using the same program and experiencing the same difficulties.

The choice of appropriate software is seldom an entirely straightforward matter, as those who have been involved in purchasing decisions relating to mainstream software such as word processing packages or spreadsheets will testify. Some software imposes a very light touch on the analyst, being confined to simple, albeit rapid, text retrieval (such as SONAR). But other packages, notably NUD•IST and ATLAS/ti, promise much more. The authors of NUD•IST explicitly claim that their software "transforms" qualitative analysis. The co-developer of ATLAS/ti has complained that, while developers have already advanced "over the horizon," users are too conservative and reluctant to use features which are technically feasible. Some other developers complain of having to remove features from their programs in order to make them accessible to qualitative researchers.

Thus, a researcher considering whether to use a package on a particular project needs to take into account the kinds of analytic work the software facilitates and the kinds of tasks for which it is unsuitable; the relevance of the features included in the software to the analytic procedures employed by different research traditions; the degree to which holistic as opposed to segmental analysis is facilitated; and the degree to which micro-analysis (e.g., conversation analysis) is facilitated. As a result, researchers usually do not decide to investigate what is available with an eye to discovering the package best suited to their needs. Rather, they have often gathered some data—in some cases quite a lot of data in qualitative terms—and look for a package as a solution. What this means is that researchers very often must learn how to use the software while their analysis is proceeding. Moreover, for younger researchers writing a thesis or embarked on their first research job, learning how to use a package and finding an appropriate style of qualitative analysis occur simultaneously.[5]

We have come to recognize that there is more in the qualitative researcher's mind than a straightforward technical choice when she or he approaches potential advisers to learn about CAQDAS. We believe it is helpful to look at this in the light of the considerable literature on presenting for assistance in health and welfare settings. Those in applied health research will be familiar with the idea that when a patient calls on the general practitioner, the doctor may well feel that the patient's "real" trouble is not the complaint which the patient identifies in requesting a consultation. In particular, GPs may be inclined to "read" some requests in psychodynamic terms. In welfare settings, social workers and probation officers have a developed rhetoric on "presenting problems." The idea is again that the problem that has led the client to present herself or himself for service may be more extensive or different in character than the reason initially given. For instance, probation officers learn to delve more deeply when clients disclose continued offending (Jarvis 1978). While the officer should formally be considering breach of the probation order when this happens, it is normal to hold breach as last resort, only to be used if the situation that is thought to have occasioned the disclosure affords the officer nothing more to work on. Likewise, social workers are inclined to differentiate "presenting problems" from those aspects of a client's situation which they regard as (1) actually causing the presenting problem, and (2) as susceptible to some approved and feasible form of social work intervention.

We feel there are parallels with potential CAQDAS users. The immediate issue may be "can CAQDAS help with my research problem?" or, often, "tell me which package to use," but it is rarely possible to address such concerns without learning quite a bit more about the person's project. Among the issues here are: how "computerate" (computer literate) is the researcher and is there a favored platform; what is the project timetable and what stage has the researcher reached; is the researcher working alone or on a team, and, in particular, who will be responsible for applying the data to the software; for what research audience is the report/publication intended; what analytic commitments and orientation does the researcher bring to the analysis? While "the tools for the job" remains our pragmatic emphasis, the general point is that we have to know quite a bit about "the job" before tools can be specified.

PROGRAMS IN THE RESEARCH ENVIRONMENT

An early preoccupation of commentaries on the implications of CAQDAS for qualitative research was a concern that the use of software would result in superficial analysis, particularly where it was done by people with little background in qualitative methods, and that the software could subtly distort analysis according to conventions built into the program design (Lee and Fielding 1991). The fear that the use of CAQDAS poses a threat of facile analyses, analyses steered in a particular direction by program conventions and features, or the loss of craft skills, does not seem realistic on the basis of experience with programs at their present level of sophistication. Based on our focus group research, we would suggest that in the long run the social context within which program development takes place is inherently pluralistic. Particular programs have particular strengths and weaknesses. However, continued contact with users—which results from the existence of a relatively non-commercialized community of users and developers—encourages developers to adapt their programs to multiple styles of use. In addition, developers have frequently demonstrated their own epistemological awareness of the problems potentially involved in program use (Seidel 1991; Richards and Richards 1991). It is also clear from our focus group material that users will cease to use a program rather than persist with unsuitable use. This is not to deny that CAQDAS poses issues which need to be negotiated and accommodated in research teams.

A particular issue is that senior members of the team may find themselves marginalized in some areas of project work due to their lack of familiarity with information technology. This is, of course, a well-remarked problem in other areas where IT has been applied. It could even be read as a subtle democratization of the team research process. In quantitatively-based research, for instance, it is quite usual for research assistants to have a superior working knowledge of software to those directing the project; we know of projects where relatively junior researchers have borne heavy responsibilities because of the unfamiliarity of the project director with statistical packages (though not, of course, with the statistics themselves). Also, in studies of epidemiology and other research in the health field, projects may be directed by people with medical expertise who rely on research officers for social research skills including computing. But senior qualitative researchers are, perhaps, particularly likely to suffer alienation from IT and to feel de-skilled and out of date. In running training courses in the use of CAQDAS we have noticed that such users are most prone to compound unfamiliarity with the basics of information technology with doubts about the desirability of entrusting parts of the analytic process to a computer. This is understandable, since those established in the field will have been trained at a time when computing applications were unknown in qualitative research.

An implication of the discussion above is that younger qualitative researchers will increasingly see an acquaintance with software for qualitative analysis as a necessary skill with which to obtain leverage in the job market. This is not just due to the aura of competence associated with the use of new technology, although this should not be discounted (see Lee and Fielding 1991). To an extent, qualitative research is a victim of its own success here. Qualitative methods have gained enhanced legitimacy in applied research in recent years, particularly in the United States. Government funding has created career opportunities for social scientists in the evaluation of federal and state programs especially in health, education, and welfare. Multimethod approaches are dominant here, so that qualitative methods have a niche. Another reason is the rediscovery of the focus group (group discussion) method and its application in market research and advertising. The place of qualitative method in academic research had been expanding for some time before, as the onslaught of various philosophical critiques of naive positivist epistemologies increasingly registered. For example, there has been a very considerable increase in the numbers of research methods textbooks specifically devoted to qualitative research; one publisher alone has produced in excess of 40 new titles in its qualitative methods list since 1986.

Further, the applied research world, including evaluation and market research, has grown more sophisticated about the limitations of analysis based purely on quantitative research. In the United States, for example, community-based, federally-funded research on AIDS has primarily been ethnographic in character (Kotarba 1990; Lee 1993), despite the traditionally quantitative character of much applied social research. Qualitative researchers were able to gain access to at-risk populations, such as prostitutes, invisible to large-scale surveys because of their social invisibility and deviant social status. In Britain the impetus on the increasing sophistication of public opinion concerning statistics may well have been the endless "revisions" to official employment data by Conservative administrations intent on minimizing the apparent depth of the recession, along with the credibility gap associated with the difference between criminal statistics and the public's daily experience of crime.

But, at least as regards government research, the improved legitimacy of qualitative research has also been prompted by the agencies and policymakers themselves, as well as public opinion. For example, the Home Office, the Police Inspectorate, and chief constables themselves, have for many years been enthusiasts for "community policing." Yet a series of official surveys show few differences between community policing and conventional patrol methods (Fielding 1993). During the late 1980s it began to be argued within these groups that perhaps those things that could be quantified could not adequately capture the reality of the phenomenon. Perhaps the best efforts of community police remained invisible to such measures. Qualitative measures were duly designed and issued (notably by the Association of Chief Police Officers and the Inspectorate).

The young researcher thus surveys a different scene from that on which applied researchers gazed even a few years ago, where there is a greater openness to qualitative methods and even a willingness to base policy decisions on studies involving qualitative methods. But it is also observable that the "conversion" of research sponsors to the legitimacy of such methods does not sweep away established emphases, such as that on generalizability and representativeness. Crudely, research sponsors read these on the basis of sample size: big is still beautiful. It may be epistemologically debatable, but the sponsors' conversion to "depth" is not associated with an abandonment of the perceived need for "range." Thus, the researcher proposing an applied study based on intensive interviews may find it easier to gain consent for the interview method, provided it is applied to at least 100 research subjects. It is for such reasons that we would suggest that competence in the use of qualitative analysis software is gaining ground as an attractive vocational skill. Summing up these considerations we would comment that the impact of software in the research environment is not a purely technical or practical matter. It also relates to the power dynamics of small working groups and the career structure of social research.

The effects of CAQDAS on research teams are, then, neither mysterious nor dissimilar to other issues of working relationships and procedures which affect small working groups. In particular, the impact of CAQDAS is affected by power relationships and organizational structure. Such relationships and structures affect data collection, quality control, and data analysis. It is in this indirect way that the use of CAQDAS has an impact on the research environment, and, through this, on the nature of the knowledge which research produces. (The matter is discussed in similar terms in another field of applied research in Cameron et al. 1992.)

It is readily accepted that technology will have an effect on work and working groups, but this is not confined to its direct effects.

For example, the development of telephone interviewing has made for new relationships between researcher and research subject. The technology enables the creation of intimacy without proximity, or even the appearance of empathy without the responsibilities such relations create in direct, face-to-face fieldwork. It is widely remarked among those engaged in such work that intimate experiences and feelings will be shared that, in their view, may not have been shared in direct fieldwork (Renzetti 1992). This disembodied intimacy is readily exploited by field-workers, and possibly by research subjects, who may feel that the medium licenses distorted or exaggerated responses. This seems to speak to several facets of the postmodern social world: new forms of intimacy, new experiences of alienation. But the technological challenge to the accepted spatial and temporal "constants" of human sociality can also revive exploitative characteristics of the "modern" industrial world.

Where telephone interviewing is conducted using computer prompting and data entry (CATI—Computer Assisted Telephone Interviewing), the opportunity arises to organize fieldwork on an industrial model, with technology affording supervisors a ready and instant check on productivity. Large research organizations using CATI organize field-workers at long rows of CATI consoles, divided by partitions from each other but patrolled from behind to discourage idle talk among operatives and maximize phone talk. Such facilities are heavily used in election polls, sales campaigns, and market research. It is obvious that telephone interviewing need not be organized in this way: the technology can be used to create a mediated intimacy where disclosure is encouraged and sensitively received, or to build a battery farm of demotivated human data sensors.

The parallel with CAQDAS in the research environment is that those who know the data best, having collected it and then processed it using the software, may have least impact on the overall direction of analysis and be least likely to gain credit for their role. Like the problems of the "postmodern," we suspect, there is nothing new in this. But we must not think that because the daily drudgery of analysis is computer-aided, the old research ethics problems do not apply, in this case, those pertaining to power relations between managers and subordinates in research teams. One particular manifestation of this is the relationship between researchers of different genders. As a research tool the computer is invested with symbolic meanings stressing its technical character and which, in other contexts, has encouraged the exclusion of women. As Lyman (1984) puts it, "while the cybernetic model [implicit in computing] may be a useful paradigm for knowledge, it is markedly different from that of qualitative research, which emphasizes diagnosis, not control, and interpretation, not explanation. In learning to use the computer the field-worker is consuming a culture of control not just a tool."

Disparities of power associated with gender cross-cut (but, often, amplify) hierarchical relations in research teams (Brannen 1988). The problem may be particularly acute in qualitative methods where there is a strong belief that those involved in data collection gain analytic insight from the fieldwork process itself. Ownership of the data, technical skill in computer-assisted qualitative data analysis, and hierarchical status levels may become confounded in the course of the research.

TEACHING AND TRAINING

Given that CAQDAS can help handle some research problems and offers some efficiencies (while stimulating more sophisticated analysis in certain cases), there is an intellectual case for including knowledge of it in the student's toolkit. There is a further incentive to train: in applied research the ability to use a package will increasingly become a marketable skill. Indeed, we have already begun to notice expertise in CAQDAS appearing as a requirement in job advertisements, as well as in departmental advertisements soliciting applications for research studentships. With regard to student support, the principal funding body for graduate study in the United Kingdom, the Economic and Social Research Council, has for several years been pressing the academic social science community to secure better completion rates for doctoral studies, where "better" is construed primarily as adhering to a three or, at most, four-year timetable (ESRC 1991). In as much as

CAQDAS promises to facilitate the handling of a kind of data which is recognized as unwieldy and requiring analytic sophistication, the software will appeal to those under a time pressure to complete their analysis for whatever reason.

Richards and Richards (1991) argue that pedagogical considerations should affect program development. At their present stage of development CAQDAS programs offer troublesome, though by no means insurmountable, barriers to self-teaching. Most of our focus group participants felt that the manuals accompanying the software were inadequate. (The tutorial material which accompanies NUD•IST was generally exempted from this charge.) Indeed, there is probably a need here for the development of self-teaching packages. The reliability of software is also a pedagogical concern. As teachers we have had negative experiences both with "stand-alone" programs which must be loaded onto individual machines and with networkable programs which did not live happily on our existing hardware configurations. A number of our focus group participants had also suffered from unexplained bugs in the program they used. Problems of this kind are frightening for computer novices and in some cases, we are quite sure, led them to abandon use of the program concerned. Even where users persevered, they often found themselves being thrown back onto local support services. In many cases this proved to be unsatisfactory. Although we are aware of sterling exceptions to the general rule, computer support staff are often not entirely helpful. CAQDAS programs are not well known outside the qualitative analysis community. Moreover, many computer support staff have backgrounds in the natural sciences or in statistics and sometimes have difficulty in relating to qualitative analysis.

As we have argued elsewhere (Lee and Fielding 1991) the teaching of qualitative research may in the longer term benefit from technological advances such as the development of CD-ROM, multimedia, the use of expert systems, intelligent simulation, and virtual reality. Related to this are issues relating to the design of the human-computer interface. There is a general trend in program design toward the use of Graphical User Interfaces which, for example, display information on-screen within movable and resizable windows and where commands can be executed through the use of menus manipulated through a pointing device such as a mouse. In our view, this trend is to be emphatically welcomed from a teaching point of view. One reason is that the vast majority of commercial programs students now encounter have such interfaces. The increasingly common "look and feel" of programs aids the learning of any one program. But these programs also aid learning to the extent that they provide intuitive ways of performing routine tasks. One of us received unexpected confirmation of this with a group of students on a masters degree course who, left to their own devices in a laboratory containing machines on which a number of CAQDAS programs were running, gravitated en masse to a machine using HyperResearch, a Macintosh-based program with a well-thought out interface based on a metaphor—the index card—familiar to qualitative researchers.

We said earlier that, in choosing CAQDAS, users will often be confronting the analysis of a particular (and large) data set at the same time as they are trying to learn the package. This raises another emphasis in our data. Respondents expressed the view that in contemporary degree courses, novice users of qualitative analysis software were usually also novices in qualitative research generally. Rather than adept ethnographers with a background in, say, anthropology, students were being introduced to packages as part of their instruction in qualitative methods. One important teaching issue is therefore whether an introduction to CAQDAS should be placed in the computing component of a degree course or in a methods component. There is great diversity here and developments are moving fast. Because we are looking at a group of users at what is still a relatively early point in the emergence of the software (with even the leading packages generally still available in early versions, and with most users having adopted CAQDAS only in the last five years), we would not expect their experiences to represent those of current students. Thus, our respondents' introduction to CAQDAS has largely been after they took up work as researchers. Current students will be entering the job market already possessing some knowledge of CAQDAS.

In these circumstances we would want to say that no one yet has the "right" answer to where software awareness sessions should be placed in a course. What we can do, however, is report our experience. We would hazard a guess that the great majority of students pursuing undergraduate social science degrees do not seek careers in social research upon graduation. Like other undergraduate degrees, it is usually the possession of a higher education qualification itself that provides leverage, rather than its subject. Those that do seek such a career will, we would guess, largely enter through a postgraduate qualification. The fresh undergraduate intent on a research career will begin by seeking further qualifications, conventionally either a specialist masters or a Ph.D., and the latter is increasingly likely to include some masters level methods training. But even here only a proportion of students will be interested in qualitative methods. Thus, at the postgraduate level, the most that courses should be expected to provide for the general run of students will be introduction and awareness sessions. A proportion will, of course, already be committed to qualitative research, or grabbed by CAQDAS as demonstrated, or both. This self-selecting group should be given the opportunity to develop competence in the use of CAQDAS by the medium of small group, hands-on teaching. If experience on Surrey's Masters in Social Research program is any guide, a further subgroup will wish to use a package to facilitate the analysis of their dissertation data. This has been the pattern over the seven years to date that qualitative analysis software has been introduced in the degree.

The vehicle for the general introduction is the two-term course in field methods, which comprises a term on data collection issues and a term on data analysis. Initially, one 90 minute session on The Ethnograph was presented in the second term (as part of a sequence on different approaches to the analysis of interview data). The session involved a description of the principal features of the package, given in lecture format, followed by the circulation of some worked print-out including examples of a line-numbered transcript, coded transcript, single sorts, and multiple sorts. A brief summary of alternative packages was included. Subsequently, two sessions have been included, the second to accommodate a demonstration of The Ethnograph with a screen display using a display tablet, and a profile of the HyperRESEARCH™ package. The summary of alternative packages has also been expanded by adding several new packages. These largely formal, lecture format presentations are backed by a voluntary attendance class in a computing laboratory. Students' hands-on forays are assisted by teaching staff and/or a technician. There is no involvement of central computing staff in any of these sessions, department staff being wholly responsible for the input. An increasing number of dissertations employ a CAQDAS package, although it remains a minority of those based on qualitative methods, and dissertation students have required little extra assistance in software aspects of their work, suggesting that the general lecture(s) and the practical class suffice to support the use of these relatively simple packages (the dissertation students have so far confined themselves to the packages taught in the course). As to where to place the CAQDAS teaching in relation to the learning of other computing skills, by the time in the degree when the CAQDAS sequence takes place the students are in the penultimate term of the six terms of their taught course, and have been working with Minitab, SPSS-PC, and a word processing package since term one. There is also a general introduction-to-computing theme in the first term data analysis course, so that Minitab and then SPSS-PC are introduced in tandem with the teaching of statistics.

An alternative strategy, at least at the undergraduate level, might recognize that increasing numbers of institutions are providing students with basic IT training as part of their undergraduate studies. It may therefore be possible to introduce CAQDAS at an introductory level as one of a range of computing strategies useful to students. This has the disadvantage of detaching program use from a wider discussion of qualitative research methods, but by the same token, it might help to avoid the ghettoization of qualitative methods which is currently commonplace in the undergraduate research methods curriculum. At Royal Holloway University of London undergraduates pursuing social science degree courses normally undertake a modular course in computer applications in the social sciences. As part of this course students are introduced first of all to structured approaches to the analysis of text of the kind common in the humanities; the use of word-counting, indexing, and concordancing programs. Students fairly readily understand the principles behind these methods since they are relatively structured. They are then introduced to CAQDAS software using both lectures and a limited hands-on introduction to The Ethnograph. Students readily see how software of this kind differs in its principles and operation from the more structured approaches they have just seen. It should be said, however, that this kind of approach has proved much less successful with postgraduates. Here, the more structured methods typical of humanities computing are regarded as extradisciplinary approaches and, as such, are perceived as a distraction.

At present, then, the message seems to be that, just as there is no "industry standard" CAQDAS package, there is great diversity in the training of qualitative researchers, the conditions under which they work and the needs they bring to decisions about which package to choose. It is a message that software developers and those who advise on software use need to bear in mind.

ACKNOWLEDGMENTS

Support for the pilot phase of this research came from the Department of Social Policy and Social Science at Royal Holloway University of London. The main part of the study is being funded by Economic and Social Research Council, Grant No. R000234586.

NOTES

1. We should point out, however, that an incidental finding of our research is that such lists actually give a rather poor idea of who is using the software. Often the registered user is, for example, a computing center staff member who often lacks a clear idea of who is using what.

2. Current developments in arts and humanities computing are most conveniently followed in the journal, *Computers in the Humanities*. Strangely, in some respects there has been relatively little cross-fertilization of ideas between computer users in the arts and humanities and social scientists.

3. The significance of this from our point of view is that funding for such events has been modest. Our conclusion seems to be that investment of this kind

does seem to be effective in encouraging the diffusion of new methods and technologies.

4. A bulletin board is essentially an electronic discussion group devoted to a particular topic. For example, sociologists in the United Kingdom can subscribe to a bulletin board ("SocBB") on which is posted information, queries, discussions of topical relevance, and so on. To subscribe, send an e-mail message to socbb-request@soc.surrey.ac.uk, saying "subscribe (your) first name, last name." Qualitative researchers worldwide have a dedicated bulletin board ("Qual-RS") located at the University of Georgia. To join, send a message to listserv@uga-.cc.uga.edu saying "subscribe qual-rs first name, last name, institution." In case of difficulty consult the electronic mail specialist in your local computing center.

5. We have occasionally found instances of researchers being encouraged to use a package by research managers who perceive in it potential efficiency or productivity gains. While we think this is quite rare at present, we suspect this kind of situation is likely to become more common.

REFERENCES

Agar, M.

1991 "The Right Brain Strikes Back." In *Using Computers in Qualitative Research*, edited by N.G. Fielding and R.M. Lee. London: Sage.

Brannen, J.

1988 "The Study of Sensitive Subjects." *Sociological Review* 36: 552-563.

Brent, E.E., Jr., and R.E. Anderson

1990 *Computer Applications in the Social Sciences*. Philadelphia: Temple University Press.

Busa, R.

1980 "The Annals of Computing: The Index Thomisticus." *Computers in the Humanities* 14(2): 83-90.

Cameron, D., E. Frazer, P. Harvey, M.B.H. Rampton, and K. Richardson.

1992 *Researching Language: Issues of Power and Method.* London: Routledge.

Choueka, Y.

1980 "Computerized Full-text Retrieval Systems and Research in the Humanities: The Responsa Project." *Computers in the Humanities* 14(2): 153-169.

ESRC Training Board

1991 *Postgraduate Training Guidelines*. Swindon, England: Economic and Social Research Council.

Fielding, N.G.

1993 "Policing and the Role of the Police." In *Reforming British Policing,* edited by R. Dingwall and J. Shapland. Sheffield, England: University of Sheffield Faculty of Law.

Glaser, B.O., and A. Strauss
1967 *The Discovery of Grounded Theory.* Chicago: Aldine.
Granovetter, M.
1973 "The Strength of Weak Ties." *American Journal of Sociology* 78: 1360-1380.
Jarvis, F.V.
1978 *The Probation Officers' Training Manual.* London: Butterworths.
Kotarba, J.
1990 "Ethnography and AIDS: Returning to the Streets." *Journal of Contemporary Ethnography* 19: 259-270.
Lee, R.M.
1993 *Doing Research on Sensitive Topics.* London: Sage.
Lee, R.M., and N.G. Fielding
1991 "Computing for Qualitative Research: Options, Problems and Potential." In *Using Computers in Qualitative Research,* edited by N.G. Fielding and R.M. Lee. London: Sage.
Lyman, P.
1984 "Reading, Writing and Word Processing: Towards a Phenomenology of the Computer Age." *Qualitative Sociology* 7(1-2): 75-89.
Morton, A.G.
1980 "The Annals of Computing: The Greek Testament." *Computers in the Humanities* 14(2): 197-200.
Renzetti, C.M.
1992 *Violent Betrayal: Partner Abuse in Lesbian Relationships.* Newbury Park, CA: Sage.
Richards, L., and T. Richards
1991 "The Transformation of Qualitative Method: Computational Paradigms and Research Processes." In *Using Computers in Qualitative Research,* edited by N.G. Fielding and R.M. Lee. London: Sage.
Seidel, J.
1989 "Facilitating a More Holistic Analysis." *Cut and Paste* 1(3): 5-6.
Seidel, J.
1991 "Methods and Madness in the Application of Computer Technology to Qualitative Data Analysis." In *Using Computers in Qualitative Research,* edited by N.G. Fielding and R.M. Lee. London: Sage.
Seidel, J.
1992 Personal Communication, October 7.
Tesch, R.
1991 "Computers and Qualitative Data II: Introduction." *Qualitative Sociology* 14(3): 225-243.

UNLEASHING FRANKENSTEIN'S MONSTER?

THE USE OF COMPUTERS IN QUALITATIVE RESEARCH

Sharlene Hesse-Biber

Computer usage within sociology is not a new phenomenon. Sociologists use computer programs for analyzing data. Most computer programs are applied to quantitative methods. Qualitative sociologists have in large part avoided the use of computer programs in the analysis of their data which primarily consists of the analysis of text (gathered through observations, documents, and interviews) for patterns and meanings. Qualitative sociologists do not usually report the actual techniques they use in their qualitative data analysis. Few have codified their techniques. (There are some exceptions: Glaser and Strauss 1967; Charmaz 1983; Strauss 1987.)

Studies in Qualitative Methodology, Volume 5, pages 25-41.

ISBN: 1-55938-902-8.

The arrival of lower-priced personal computers and their portability made the computer available to the qualitative researcher in the field and office. At present there is a great demand for software programs for microcomputers. Yet there is a fear as well as promise concerning the use of computerized technology applied to qualitative research, not unlike the fear of Frankenstein's monster.

Mary Shelley's novel, *Frankenstein*, was published in 1818 and reflects the dramatic revolutionary changes in England between 1789 and 1832 during which the working class was asserting its right to vote and the country as a whole was moving from a preindustrial small-scale agricultural community to a large-scale industrial economy. In many ways, Frankenstein's monster was a symbol of revolutionary change with its accompanying destruction and promise of a new beginning. Those in power feared the working class with its lack of "traditions" would "take over" and become uncontrollable if given the vote such that chaos and instability would reign over English society (Smith 1992, pp. 3-17). Victor Frankenstein describes his creation in the following way:

> ... I suddenly beheld the figure of a man, at some distance, advancing towards me with superhuman speed. He bounded over the crevices in the ice, among which I had walked with caution; his stature, also, as he approached, seemed to exceed that of man. I was troubled: a mist came over my eyes, and I felt a faintness seize me. ... I perceived, as the shape came nearer ... that it was the wretch whom I had created. I trembled with rage and horror. ... (Shelley as quoted in Smith 1992, p. 89).

The fear Victor Frankenstein experiences coming face to face with his monster is often involved in the researcher's relationship to the computer. Just as Frankenstein's monster was held in awe and fear, there is a strong feeling among some qualitative researchers that while computers have the potential to revolutionize the field, there is also the possibility for things to run out of control. A range of fears are expressed as the researcher first begins to consider and proceeds to use computer technology to do qualitative work. This paper outlines five fears critics express concerning the use of computer software programs for qualitative data analysis.

I. ART VERSUS TECHNOLOGY

There exists the fear that machine technology will separate the qualitative researcher from the creative process. For some analysts, the experience of doing qualitative work is more comparable to artistic work. Just as the artist prefers a brush or pencil and paper, so too do some qualitative researchers. Machine technology seems incompatible or inconsistent with art. There is a strong fear that the technology will turn the researcher into an unthinking and unfeeling human being. Some qualitative researchers have commented on how much they like to work with paper or to be able to write in the margins of their interviews (see Richards and Richards 1989). Others describe the process as "mystical," "private," or "idiosyncratic" (Conrad and Reinharz 1984). There is a sense that the machine will turn research into a commodity. With the additional qualitative software features of hypothesis generation and testing of hypotheses which are now available on some computer software programs, there is the additional fear of "data dredging"—and an over reliance on technology to do one's thinking by simply having the software relate code categories automatically, using very little theoretical insight.

II. BLURRING THE LINE BETWEEN QUANTITATIVE AND QUALITATIVE ANALYSIS

Computer software programs automate the organizing, indexing, and retrieving of documents, to generate counts of occurrence of codes or concepts on data which can then be input into a statistical software package. Some critics feel that these software features may serve to blur the line between qualitative and quantitative data analysis. For many of the new software programs, there is no limit on the size of the data they can handle or the number of files. The volume of data now collected for some qualitative studies is comparable to quantitative research and there is the potential fear that qualitative research will be reduced to quantitative research. Qualitative researchers' emphasis on volume is of concern for a variety of reasons.

A. Fear of Imposing the Logic of Survey Research onto Qualitative Research

Qualitative researchers may impose the logic of general survey research and increase their sample size in hopes of generalizing their results to some empirical universe. Yet, generalizations made by qualitative researchers derive from a different logic. They are not generalizing about content but are looking to discover underlying patterns or forms within their data that have applicability to a whole range of different contexts. The logic of survey research, on the other hand, often requires that the size of the sample meet certain statistical inference issues such as needing "x" number of cases to ensure that one's results are significant at the $p = 0.05$ or $p = 0.01$ level. These assumptions about numbers are driven by the need to form empirical generalizations. Some qualitative researchers lose sight of this point when they become fixated on volume. Qualitative analysis is driven by a need to make analytical generalizations. Howard Becker (Becker 1953) studies marijuana users, not to generalize about marijuana users, but to study a process of getting involved in a deviant subculture. Numbers are important, but they are based on theoretical considerations, such as the level of saturation of code categories. According to Strauss (1987), "theoretical saturation" occurs when additional analysis no longer contributes to the discovering anything new about a category" (p. 21). A researcher needs to study more cases until he or she is not learning anything new.

B. Sacrificing In-depth Analysis to Meet High Volume Standards

Wanting to become more quantitative by focusing more on volume means that a qualitative researcher may sacrifice in-depth analysis of data in order to pursue high volume analysis. John Seidel describes this development as one symptom of "analytic madness" (Seidel 1991, p. 107) and suggests that volumes of data "will drive the analysis" and may result in a researcher "missing interesting and important things in the data" (p. 109). Ironically, the very features of computer software programs which help to computerize the process of coding, retrieving, and sorting of data can also serve to limit the type of in-depth data analysis characteristic of qualitative work.

III. DICTATING THE DEFINITION OF A FIELD AND TYPE OF QUALITATIVE DATA ANALYSIS

Michael Agar (1991) and others (Seidel 1991), caution that computer programs may dictate the very definition of a particular field of study. Agar notes the following concerning the field of ethnography:

> As more and more colleagues acquired computer know how, I heard less about what ethnography was and how to think about it, and more about the newest hardware and software and what it could do, about memory capacity and hard disk access, about the latest laptop and illuminated screen. I worried that the means was beginning to replace the end, that the comfortable certainty of bytes and baud might replace the ambiguities of indeterminate pattern and emergent research. ... The computer had shifted, in my worst-case scenario, from an aid in doing ethnography to a definition of what ethnography might do (Agar 1991, p. 182).

Computer software program structures often set requirements for how a research project should proceed. This raises concerns among some critics that computer software programs will determine the types of questions asked and the specific data analysis plan:

> Thus, we continually refer to computer-assisted qualitative research to emphasize that the computer should be used to enhance, not control, the work of the investigator. While we should take advantage of the computer's abilities, we should not let our analyses hinge primarily on what a particular software program can do. ... If we compute first and think later we may

> well lose the essence of qualitative sociological work (Conrad and Reinharz 1984, p. 10).

Horney and Healey (1991) have also made this point in a recent paper which compares two different computer programs for analyzing qualitative data. They analyzed a single data set using two different computerized software programs. They conclude:

> Computers change the nature of how data are interpreted and different programs provide different points of view. This is at odds with the common opinion that efficiency is the primary benefit computers bring to the research process. ... An analysis task thus needs to be matched with the researchers' familiarity with a program and with its metaphors (Horney and Healey 1991, p. 12).

IV. MAKING THE RESEARCHER MORE ACCOUNTABLE

Another controversy with the computerization of qualitative data is the issue of validity and reliability of the data gathered. Validity refers to whether a measure is actually measuring what a researcher thinks it is measuring. Reliability refers to whether or not the measure produces the same result each time it is used to measure the same thing. For many qualitative researchers the way one measures validity is often stated somewhat vaguely: Validity is "how closely one comes to capturing the lives of the people they study"; others talk about "how well a researcher respects the nature of the empirical world." Strauss (1987, p. 258) addresses the issue of validity still another way. In answering a question concerning how much confidence a researcher should have in their analysis he states:

> Even experienced researchers may not always be certain before they have chewed on their suspended pencils long enough to know where precisely are the holes—or be certain that, after review, they know there are no important holes—in their analyses. Whether experienced or inexperienced, a common tactic for reducing uncertainty is "the trial"—try it out on other people, individuals, or groups, informally or formally (p. 260).

Little work is published on formal validation or reliability of research works by independent observers within qualitative research. Without a formal language for describing the reasoning chain from the codes to the researcher's conclusion, many possible interpretations can lead to the same conclusions. This makes the process of independent verification even harder.

Computer programs hold out the promise and peril of enabling qualitative researchers to answer the question of how confident they are in their analysis (i.e., Do they really have their core categories right? Are their categories detailed?). Computer programs for analyzing qualitative data require the researcher to be more explicit in the procedures and analytical processes they went through to produce their data and their interpretations. The inclusion of artificial intelligence technologies into some qualitative analysis tools will ultimately allow faster, more detailed, and more verifiable coding. Asking qualitative researchers to be more explicit about their method and holding their interpretations accountable to tests of validity and reliability will raise some controversies: Should there be strict tests of validity and reliability for qualitative data? Are we again imposing the logic of quantitative measurement requirements onto qualitative data? What standards for validity and reliability should be used in qualitative research, if any?

Being more explicit about the procedures used to analyze data can make secondary analysis/replication of research studies of qualitative data more possible. At present, it is difficult to follow the exact methodology used in many qualitative studies. If procedures are made more detailed such that secondary analyses are possible, several issues may arise: How do we resolve differences in interpretation of the same data? Whose interpretation is correct? Are several interpretations possible? If so, under what conditions is this true?

The use of artificial intelligence technology will support the researcher in theory generation by allowing many more propositions to be tested in a shorter time period. The ability of some computer software programs to ascertain quickly the number of cases which support a hypothesis or set of hypotheses raises several issues, including: Will some researchers use the hypothesis tester as a data dredger? The hypothesis testing potential of some computer software programs may require qualitative researchers to contend with what up to now has been largely avoided—namely, the establishment of something akin to "significance" levels for qualitative analysis. Most qualitative researchers have been using the terms "some," "many," or "few" to signify when a theme is prevalent or not prevalent in their data. One might now ask: In how many cases did the hypothesis hold up? Should a qualitative researcher apply significance tests to qualitative data? When, if at all, is this appropriate? In asking such questions are we not, again applying the logic of quantitative research onto qualitative research? Some qualitative researchers would argue that even the single occurrence of a given phenomenon can be theoretically important (see Seidel 1991, p. 113). The fact that this theme is not supported quantitatively by the data is applying the logic of quantitative analysis to qualitative data.

V. LOSS OF CONFIDENTIALITY: THE USE OF MULTIMEDIA DATA

Some new computer software programs support the analysis of multimedia materials such as audio, video, and graphics. While the inclusion of multimedia especially the analysis of audio, video, and graphic materials allows for a much more comprehensive analysis of the data, there are important ethical problems involved in working with these data, especially with visual data. Steven Gold (1989) has taken the lead in discussing ethical issues in visual field work and I would like to present some of the ethical dilemmas he sees as important to consider. Sociologists have used the principle of confidentiality to protect respondents. This is done by ensuring that research results are not associated with any individual, group setting, or organization. Analyzing audio and visual data makes it more difficult for the researcher to ensure the confidentiality of individuals who participate in research gathering. What if someone recognizes a respondent? What if data is lost or stolen? There are also negative unintended consequences of utilizing visual data in qualitative analysis. For example, Gold points out that the circulation of photographs may result in collective harm to a group by promoting negative stereotypes. He notes this problem in a study he conducted:

> I confronted this problem in the course of studying a Vietnamese refugee community. Photographs of refugees' apartments show expensive possessions, such as television sets or stereo and video equipment, which have been collectively purchased in order to consume native-language media. Certain viewers have seen in these images a justification for the claim made by xenophobes that immigrants are "welfare chizzlers" who buy luxury items with government handouts (Gold 1989, p. 101).

The researcher needs to carefully consider the range of confidentiality issues involved when working with multimedia data. The example of the Vietnamese refugee community cited by Gold suggests that the researcher needs to be aware of the unintended interpretation of multimedia data and how easy it is for such data to be misinterpreted.

TO WHAT DEGREE ARE THE FEARS CONCERNING COMPUTER SOFTWARE PROGRAMS FOR QUALITATIVE DATA ANALYSIS JUSTIFIED?

As a developer of a new computer software program, HyperRESEARCH™,[1] for analyzing qualitative data analysis, I would like to address some of the fears critics express concerning the use of computers to analyze qualitative data.

Becoming a proactive user is vital in overcoming many of the fears analysts express in utilizing computer software. Each researcher must decide how and under what circumstances this technology will be employed in their research project. In the novel, *Frankenstein*, the monster pleads with his master not detest, fear, and spurn the creature he created:

> Remember, thou has made me more powerful than thyself; my height is superior to thine. Oh, Frankenstein be not equitable to every other, and trample upon me alone, to whom thy justice, and even thy clemency and

> affections is most due. Remember, that I am thy creature. ... (Shelley quoted in Smith 1992, p. 92).

Lee and Fielding (1991) suggest the problem with computer program technology lies in their misapplication:

> Like the monster, the programs are misunderstood. The programs are innocent of guile. It is their misapplication which poses the threat. It was exposure to human depravity which made a threat of Frankenstein's creation. Equally, the untutored use of analysis programs can certainly produce banal, unedifying and off-target analysis. But the fault would lie with the user (1991, p. 8).

The view here is that the researcher becomes entrapped by the machine technology. Pfaffenberger (1988) suggests a simple rule of thumb for assessing the researcher's degree of involvement with the computer:

> When the microcomputer starts to loom larger in significance than the original goals of the research, when it demands less engagement in the research data and more engagement in the computer, the time has come to reflect on these goals and to re-establish contact with the values and commitments that initially motivated your engagement with the human social world (pp. 23-24).

It is also important to understand the limitations of each computer software program so that the program structure does not entirely dictate the type of analysis planned. Horney and Healey (1991) note that rather than being a liability, the diversity of program structures can often provide the researcher with the opportunity for different perspectives on their data and will permit "triangulation" of research results. Triangulation is a method whereby different research methods are used to test the same finding. It is possible that a given researcher can utilize several different software programs each of which has its particular strengths and weaknesses. A multiple software design holds the promise of enhancing the validity of research findings.

Computer software programs also lessen the labor intensive aspects of doing qualitative analysis. This is not a trivial issue for the qualitative analyst. Most qualitative researchers still analyze pages of text by cutting, pasting, and filing, using scissors and a typewriter or word processor to arrange the material physically into coded groups on paper. The process of photocopying multiple copies of text, cutting them up into coded passages, and then manually retrieving the coded text takes a great many hours, days, or even weeks. Software programs for qualitative analysis also speed up the coding and retrieval process. As an example, in the software program I co-developed for analyzing qualitative data, HyperRESEARCH™, analyzing text can be accomplished by typing the original interviews, articles, or other materials into a favorite word processor or more sophisticated means can be used such as optical character recognition using scanners. Once the material for a subject has been entered into a text file, the researcher can instruct HyperRESEARCH™ to associate that text file with a given "case." The researcher can then display the text file and select portions of text on the computer screen in a manner similar to highlighting a passage of text on paper with a colored highlighter pen. The researcher then assigns a code to the selected (highlighted) text. A code is a name (or label) that points to, or acts as a reference to, the highlighted text. The code is stored on a computerized equivalent of an index card. There is one index card per case. This is analogous to the researcher actually writing a code next to the highlighted paper passage and then recording the code on a 3" x 5" index card with reference to where and in what document it appears. The researcher repeats this coding process for each case in the research study. Each case's index card can contain codes from any number of different source files. A researcher may also code her or his own comments and observations about a given case. For example, a given research project may consist of 20 test subjects (cases). For each of these 20 cases, the researcher has a transcribed interview, a self-evaluation, a questionnaire, and their own "memos" about the subject (the researcher's comments). All these materials can be kept in distinct files and imported into HyperRESEARCH™ and coded in any order.

A useful feature of HyperRESEARCH™, is the Code List, which contains all the codes used so far. This master list of codes may be manipulated in several ways and is ideally suited for more focused coding. Codes may be deleted, copied, or renamed. Any manipulation performed on a master code automatically affects all specific instances of the code on all index cards. Deleting removes the selected code and its "pointer." Copying a code is very useful when combining similar codes and allows researchers to copy the reference associated with one code (e.g., the pointer to the original text) to a new entry on the index card under the new code name.

By automating the time-consuming labor-intensive aspects of doing qualitative work, that is, the time it takes to code, index, retrieve, and store data, allows the researcher to concentrate on the generation and testing of theory. The inclusion of multimedia especially the analysis of audio, video, and graphic materials in some software programs such as HyperRESEARCH™ allows for a much more comprehensive analysis of qualitative data and provides the researcher with a fuller understanding of social context, than only analyzing text would. To code an audio tape or video disc using HyperRESEARCH™, a segment of audio or video is viewed or listened to, and the beginning and ending points are "marked" by the researcher. Beginning and ending points can be marked with the press of a button. The marked segment of the audio or video source is assigned a code, just like a segment of a text file. The system adds the new code to the index card list and remembers how to replay the selected audio or video clip. This allows the researcher to directly code original source materials and avoid possible transcription errors. In addition, visual or tonal aspects of an interview such as the mood or posture of the interviewee can now be coded. However, the researcher is not required in any way to use multimedia sources. Each of the coding systems is independent, yet each function interacts with the researcher in the same manner.[2]

Devault (1990) notes how important it is to listen to the language of the interview rather than only analyzing a transcription (text) of that same interview. In a study she conducted on women's experience with housework, she notes that the language women use to convey their experiences often lies in the hesitation with which they state something. She notes that often seemingly trivial passages of transcribed text hide the richness of the data:

> Often, I believe, this halting, hesitant, tentative talk signals the realm of not-quite-articulated experience and find where standard vocabulary is inadequate, and where a respondent tries to speak from experience and finds language wanting. I tried to listen most carefully to this kind of talk (Devault 1990, p. 103).

Because qualitative research relies so heavily on the analysis of textual material, there may be a tendency for some qualitative researchers to mainly quote respondents who are most articulate in an interview. This may have the unintended consequence of biasing results toward the more articulate group (and that group which the researcher may identify with). The availability of some software programs to easily code, retrieve, and analyze multimedia source material may breakdown this tendency and increase the representativeness of meaning among a diverse group of respondents if both verbal and non-verbal behaviors are analyzed.

In addition the ability of some software programs to analyze visual material (pictures, photographs graphics) as well as video will also help to expand the field known as "visual sociology." Visual sociology is defined as "the use of photographs, film, and video to study society and the study of visual artefacts of a society" (Harper 1989, p. 81). Visual sociology can take advantage of the technology we have developed and apply it to visual methods. As Harper notes:

> Computers, which many consider an antagonistic technology to the camera, may make it easier to use visual data in sociological research. Microcomputers can now digitalize images ..., and they can be stored in conventional electronic files and easily integrated into text, graph, or other files (Harper 1989, p. 94).

At present it is largely underdeveloped and marginal to the sociology discipline. The teaching of visual sociology would be greatly enhanced by the use of multimedia software programs.

Some computer software programs also enhance the analyst's ability to generate and test theory. The HyperRESEARCH™ software program, for example, allows a researcher to test propositions by performing Boolean searches on any code or combination of codes via the use of an expert system. The program also allows for hypothesis testing using artificial intelligence. The Expert System software technology developed by HyperRESEARCH™, for example, uses production rules to provide a semiformal mechanism for theory building and description of the inference process used to draw conclusions from the data which allows for the testing of the reliability and validity of data.

It is also important to recognize that computer-assisted programs begin to question the standard ways of doing qualitative research. This is evident in the controversy surrounding the discussion on issues of quantification, validity, and reliability. Quantifying qualitative data can enhance its validity only if one is careful about how this is carried out. Counting themes or categories in the data always needs to be linked to the respondents own method of ordering the world (gathered from qualitative analysis). As Silverman (1985) notes:

> The aim is not to count for counting's sake, but in order to establish a thoughtful dialogue with qualitatively-derived insights about the setting and actors' version of the situation at hand (p. 148).

By quantifying, the analyst can assess the representativeness of the data as a whole. Researchers will be able to tighten their analysis and perhaps specify more clearly the application of their research findings to the data (Silverman 1985).

The issue of whether the computer will impose inappropriate validity/reliability standards on the qualitative analyst or if such standards are appropriate still needs to be carefully addressed among qualitative analysts. There also remains the concern as to whether or not some advanced techniques used in quantitative data analysis such as hypothesis testing and more elaborate statistical procedures can be added on to qualitative data analysis without profoundly changing the basic nature of qualitative work.

Computers hold out the promise of revolutionizing the way researchers conduct their analysis, but they also hold out a set of caveats for the qualitative analyst. The researcher who uses these programs should assess their strengths and weaknesses as well as the implications of using computer software programs to analyze qualitative data. It is clear that the interpretation of qualitative data is enriched by the use of computer software programs and that more dialogue is needed on other issues before the fear of Frankenstein's monster is put to rest.

NOTES

1. HyperRESEARCH™ is distributed by Researchware Inc., 20 Soren Street Randolph, MA 02368-1945, USA. Telepone number: (617) 961-3909.
2. For a more detailed description of all the features of the HyperRESEARCH™ software program please refer to Hesse-Biber, Dupuis, and Kinder (1991).

REFERENCES

Agar, M.
1991 "The Right Brain Strikes Back." In *Using Computers in Qualitative Research*, edited by N.G. Fielding and R.M. Lee. Newbury Park, CA: Sage Publications.

Becker, H.S.
1953 "Becoming a Marihuana User." *American Journal of Sociology* 59: 235-242.

Charmaz, K.
1983 "The Grounded Theory Method: An Explication and Interpretation." In *Contemporary Field Research: A Collection of Readings*, edited by R.M. Emerson. Prospect Heights, IL: Waveland Press, Inc.

Conrad, P., and S. Reinharz
1984 "Computers and Qualitative Data: Editor's Introductory Essay." *Qualitative Sociology* 7(1-2): 3-15.

Devault, M.
1990 "Feminist Interviewing and Analysis." *Social Problems* 37(1): 96-116.

Glaser, B.G., and A.L. Strauss
1967 *The Discovery of Grounded Theory: Strategies for Qualitative Research.* Chicago: Aldine.

Gold, S.J.
1989 "Ethical Issues in Visual Field Work." Pp. 99-109 in *New Technology in Sociology: Practical Applications in Research and Word*, edited by G. Blank, J.L. McCartney, and E. Brent. New Brunswick, NJ: Transaction Publishers.

Harper, D.
1989 "Visual Sociology: Expanding Sociological Vision." Pp. 81-97 in *New Technology in Sociology: Practical Applications in Research and Works*, edited by G. Blank, J.L. Mc Cartney, and E. Brent. New Brunswick, NJ: Transaction Publishers.

Hesse-Biber, S., P. Dupuis, and T.S. Kinder
1991 "HyperRESEARCH: A Computer Program for the Analysis of Qualitative Data with an Emphasis on Hypothesis Testing and Multimedia Analysis." *Qualitative Sociology* 14(4): 289-306.

Horney, M.A., and D. Healey
1991 "Hypertext and Database Tools for Qualitative Research." Paper Presented at the American Education Research Association (AERA), Chicago, IL., April.

Lee, R.M., and N.G. Fielding
1991 "Computing for Qualitative Research: Options, Problems and Potential." Pp.1-13 in *Using Computers in Qualitative Research*, edited by N.G. Fielding and R.M. Lee. Newbury, CA: Sage Publications.

Pfaffenberger, B.
1988 *Microcomputer Applications in Qualitative Research.* Newbury Park, CA: Sage Publications.

Richards, L., and T. Richards
1989 "The Impact of Computer Techniques for Qualitative Analysis." Technical Report, no. 6189, Department of Computer Science, La Trobe University.

Seidel, J.
1991 "Method and Madness in the Application of Computer Technology to Qualitative Data Analysis." Pp. 107-116 in *Using Computers in Qualitative Research*, edited by N.G. Fielding and R.M. Lee. Newbury Park: CA.: Sage Publications.

Silverman, D.
1985 *Qualitative Methodology and Sociology.* Hants, England: Gower Publishing Co. Ltd.

Smith, J.M. (Ed).
1992 *Mary Shelley, Frankenstein.* Boston, MA: St. Martin's Press.

Strauss, A.L.
1987 *Qualitative Analysis for Social Scientists.* New York: Cambridge University Press.

QUALITATIVE ANALYSIS AND MICROCOMPUTER SOFTWARE:

SOME REFLECTIONS ON A NEW TREND IN SOCIOLOGICAL RESEARCH[1]

Wilma Mangabeira

The 1980s can be regarded as a turning point in the increase in use of computers in the social sciences. With the introduction of the relatively inexpensive and "user-friendly" IBM-PC and its clones, social scientists expanded their use of computers beyond statistical analysis to encompass computers for text management, field-work, computer "conferencing," raw data access, and teaching.

This expansion in the role of computers is now being accompanied by the emergence of computer software and knowledge-based systems designed to handle *qualitative data*. The end of the 1980s marked the closing of an era when computer

Studies in Qualitative Methodology, Volume 5, pages 43-62.

ISBN: 1-55938-902-8.

software was the exclusive terrain of quantitative research and computers could only deal with numerical data.

A definition of "qualitative data" is difficult to formulate since there are competing concepts which vary according to the sociological approach adopted (Halfpenny 1979, p. 806). For the purposes of this paper, I will retain a largely methodological definition. Thus by qualitative data I refer to data which is non-numerical, unstructured, and of variable length. This data may be obtained through a variety of research methods including, for example, unstructured or semi-structured interviews, participant observation, and the collection of life histories.

This paper will address two related questions regarding a new trend in which qualitative researchers are making progressively more use of software for computer-assisted analysis of text. First, I will illustrate the possibilities of computer-assisted analysis through a personal account of the use of The Ethnograph software, in my own Ph.D. research. Second, I will discuss the implications of this new trend, both for sociological paradigms and for everyday research practice.[2]

I will argue that the use of computer software for the analysis of qualitative data is an important breakthrough for sociological research, since it enhances the speed of the analysis, as well as the freedom to "play with the data" and explore different possibilities of data interpretation. Furthermore it allows for the advancement of comparative work, given its systematic system of classification and retrieval of data. On the other hand, I also argue that if this new trend in not sufficiently debated, it may, in the near future, give rise some undesirable results.

This paper is divided into three sections. In the first part, I present the historical background of the penetration of computers in the social sciences and comment on what I see as the latest phase in this process, namely the emergence of computer programs designed for qualitative analysis.

In the second part of the paper I will illustrate the possibilities of a particular software package called The Ethnograph, using my Ph.D. research based on fieldwork among steelworkers in Rio de Janeiro, Brazil. My aim will be to demonstrate the advantages of the use of computer programs for qualitative research as compared with traditional manual analysis.

In the concluding part of the paper, I will assess the positive and negative implications of this new development for sociological research.

THE USE OF COMPUTERS IN SOCIAL SCIENCE: HISTORICAL BACKGROUND AND MAJOR TRENDS

The use of computers in the social sciences can be traced back to the late 1950s when attention began to focus on the development of computer-supported methodologies for the humanities. Computers were used primarily, if not exclusively, for statistical purposes and the mainframe computer was the predominant form of hardware.[3] Although there are references to the use of the mainframe computer in the humanities—especially in archaeology and language studies—the high costs of operation and the highly unfriendly environment of mainframes, deterred "computer illiterate" researchers (for details see Patton and Holoien 1981).

In the 1970s, the reduction of costs to a point where mainframe computers became accessible to many colleges and university researchers led to the development of more specific packages for the social sciences. A prime example of this process was the advent of the Statistical Package for the Social Sciences (SPSS), which became widely used in quantitative research. The introduction of database technology also expanded the usefulness of the computer as a tool for the social sciences. Nevertheless, the community of computer-users remained small.

It was in the early 1980s—with the micro-electronics revolution—that the computer shrank in size, became a consumer good, and had its price decrease. Computer hardware moved quickly away from mainframes to micro-computers.[4] The advent of the cheap, generic software packages that followed brought social scientists closer to the computer. The management of files, word processing packages, bibliographical databases, and a whole range of computer communication facilities, allowed social scientists to use computers more freely, irrespective of their methodological orientation.[5]

Up to this time, qualitative researchers who had resisted, quite correctly in my view, the "numericization" of their qualitative data were marginalized from the computer. It is fair to say that until very recently the "non-computer type" was mainly to be found among qualitative researchers, reinforcing to a certain extent the stereotyped behavior attributed to both "qualitative" and "quantitative" researchers. The advent of accessible PCs and a wide variety of word processing packages began to break down this division and many qualitativists became "computer literate." In relation to *data analysis*, however, software was still limited to numerically coded and highly structured data. There have been creative accounts of adaptation of general database managers to qualitative data analysis, in which the "coding" and "searching" of textual and unstructured data is accomplished (for interesting examples see Evans and Bernard 1983; Gerson 1986). Nevertheless, database managers can be regarded as a step behind the capabilities of the specially designed software packages.

The adaptation of general purpose database management to qualitative data analysis suffers from two main limitations. First, database managers require an initial investment of time and computer skills (even if limited) from the researcher in order to input the specific research data in line with the computer software. Second, database managers usually limit the coding or indexing process to words rather than segments of text. They also do not allow for "nested" codes or for overlapping boundaries between segments of text.

By contrast, when using specially designed software for qualitative analysis, the researcher only has to input his or her data into the program before running it. In addition to the fact that these programs allow for the coding of whole segments of text, the context of the codes are kept together in a search, and thus a very important feature of the interpretation of qualitative data is respected. In conclusion, the major advantage of specially designed software for qualitative data over general purpose database managers is that qualitative data is appropriately treated in relation to its form and content.

Computer programs designed specially for non-numerical data can be divided into two categories. One type includes software created specifically for the coding and code searching of qualitative data. According to Fielding (1993), there are at least 15 software programs of this type currently available (for descriptions of some of these programs see Fielding 1993; Tesch 1990). Although they vary greatly in terms of special features, they all replace the basic manual activity implied in the analysis of qualitative data: the cutting and pasting of text. Another common feature of these programs is that they have all, with very few exceptions, been produced by qualitative researchers, with varying degrees of computer skills.

The second type of computer program for qualitative analysis belongs to the "expert-system branch of artificial intelligence (AI)." These expert-systems are capable of interpreting or ascribing some meaning to a text or making simulations in accordance with pre-specified rules (Hinze 1987; Sproull and Sproull 1982). In contrast to both the commercialized general software which has a multiplicity of uses inside and outside the social sciences, and the "qualitative analysis programmes" described above, these expert-system programs are usually purpose-designed by computer scientists for a particular analysis in institutional projects.[6] Since this paper focuses on computer programs of the first type, I will present in the next section an illustration of a particular software and discuss its use.

THE ETHNOGRAPH SOFTWARE AND ITS USE IN A PH.D. THESIS

"The Ethnograph"[7] is a computer software package which belongs to the first group of programs outlined above. It was created by Seidel, Kjolseth, and Seymour, all themselves qualitative researchers. The software replaces the traditional "cut and paste" activity at that point in the research where all the interviews and/or field observations have been transcribed and organized, and thorough analysis should begin.

Traditionally, one would begin indexing or coding the data by making multiple copies of the material and literally "cutting and pasting" the material by categories. The basic procedure for starting work with The Ethnograph program is to have the transcribed material and/or the fieldwork notes typed into a computer word processing package. Each file of the textual data is then imported into The Ethnograph by a conversion feature. This new file is called an *Ethno File* or a *Data File*, and is only a copy of the original text file, which is left undisturbed, in its word processing format.

In this conversion process, the renaming of the original file may be also used as a device for data protection and the maintenance of the anonymity of the informants.

By running the "number the files" procedure, the program then numbers all the data files, one by one, from the first line of text (number 1) to the last line of text (which can be up to line 9999).

The Ethnograph then produces a printout of these files—that is, a printed copy of the original file with each line numbered and a space of 3 inches in the right hand margin for the researcher's notes and codes.

The software does not allow for the input of comments into the original body of the files, once they have been turned into an Ethno or Data File. All alterations and notes must be made either in the original text file before conversion to the program, or on a separate sheet of paper. Since the process of commenting on the data is itself one form of analysis, the "inflexibility" of The Ethnograph in this respect, constitutes a limitation of the program.

With the printout of the "numbered files," the data is ready for the coding process, which represents the first step of the analytical process within the program.

To "make sense" of the data, the researcher must leave the computer, take the printouts and think over the data in a more "traditional fashion," that is, with pencil and paper. Thus, although the program was created in order to eliminate the mechanical tasks of qualitative research, the initial analytical interaction between "researcher" and "data" is through a manual procedure.

This is a specific feature of The Ethnograph and was intentionally produced by its creators. According to Seidel "the researcher has to be involved in the manipulation of the data in order to stay in touch with it" (Seidel et al. 1988, pp. 1-3). This feature was welcomed by some users but also criticized by others.

Because of my personal style of working, I identified greatly with it since I benefited from being able to undertake a thorough and comparative "reading" of the printouts. However, this is a very individual option; other researchers might prefer the coding process to occur on the computer screen, directly over the text.

Once the researcher has completed this first manual coding process, he or she can return to the computer and input the codes with their respective segments of text. The numbers in the printout make it possible for segments of text to be referenced to one specific code or various codes. The input of codes into the program is achieved by running the "code a file" option and inputting the code word or words at the appropriate line numbers of segments of text.

The program is sophisticated enough to allow each segment of text to have up to 12 different codes. Different segments of text can also overlap or nest with each other up to seven times.[8] The recoding process of the data file is very simple. The program allows for changes in the numbering of the segments of text, in the names of the codes, as well as the addition of new codes.

During the input of the codes of the respective data files into the program, the researcher is completely separated from the text. The computer screen works as a "blank" page, which is filled in by codes and line numbers. This has been criticized by some, who argue that through this procedure, the context of the coding might be lost (Conference on Qualitative Knowledge and Computing, July 1989).

Once again, this depends on the researcher's personal style of work. I myself found that this method of coding helped me to detach myself intellectually from the original material. Altogether, the context of the code is only momentarily lost, to be regained in the searching procedure and the printout of the results. In reference to this, The Ethnograph offers two possibilities of printout, called "large picture" or "small picture." In other words, the program offers the possibility of a variable display of the context of the codes (Seidel et al. 1988, pp. 9-24).

I subscribe to the idea that the coding process is the culmination of two movements that occur simultaneously in the analytical process. On the one hand, the researcher should have "grown old with his data," to cite Seidel's expression, which indicates the need for the researcher to be deeply familiar with his or her field material. On the other hand, the researcher should also be able to detach himself from the original data, so that some level of summarizing and abstraction can occur.

As Sproull and Sproull (1982, p. 284) have suggested, in order for the researcher to make some summary statement or describe recurring patterns, he or she "categorizes" the original records. With this, the categories themselves, their recurrences, overlappings, and nestings become the data that is used in the analysis. The original and complete material is put aside to be used in the written text, as "illustrations."

In The Ethnograph, the "search a code" process can begin after the data files have been coded and recoded and the researcher is reasonably satisfied with the code mapping of the data. The "heart" of the software is the search process when the researcher can "play" with the multiple possibilities of data interpretation, in the search for meanings, patterns, and regularities. The program allows for both single code searching and multiple code searching, for parts or all of the data files. In multiple code searching, up to five code words can be used, selected by "and" and "not."

The search process can be enriched by another feature called "face-sheets" which allow for much more complex analytical possibilities. However, before describing this in detail, I would like to present a general view of my own research so that it can be used in the illustration of the program.

THE RESEARCH THESIS—MAIN QUESTIONS

The thesis is titled *Union Politics and Workplace Militancy: A Case Study of Brazilian Steelworkers in the 1980s* (Mangabeira 1991). The thesis analyzes the relationship between shop-floor militancy and union politics in the period after the birth of "new unionism" in Brazil in the 1980s and addresses the problems and dilemmas faced by this new type of union movement.

The objectives of the thesis were twofold. First, it offered an in-depth study of the relationship between shop-floor politics and union politics in a steel plant. The second objective was to assess the developments of "new unionism" in Brazil, 10 years after its birth and to discuss the extent to which it has actually broken with populist and bureaucratic types of unionism and advanced toward more democratic forms of union politics.

One of the aims proclaimed by the "new unionist" union was that the two levels of industrial activism—the union and the shop-floor—should be closely related to each other. This principal was questioned by the thesis. Indeed the major focus of the thesis was around the issue of union democracy and the extent to which the rank and file became adequately represented by the "new unionist" union. My analytical frame of reference is based on two theoretical perspectives: namely, the debate on union democracy found within political sociology and inaugurated by Robert Michels (1959) and Burawoy's concept of "politics of production" (1987) found within the labor process debate.

This thesis on political sociology took up the "new unionist" debate and attempted to assess how its general characteristics developed in the past 10 years. Since the "new unionist" movement was defined by the literature as "new" within the Brazilian labor movement due to its greater militancy and by the greater representativeness of its leadership, the starting point of the thesis was a redefinition of *union politics* to encompass two areas of industrial collective action, namely *the union* and the *shop-floor*.[9] The first area of analysis concentrated on the formal and institutionalized relationship between manual workers as a rank and file and their union leadership. The second area of analysis was that of shop-floor politics, where focus is drawn, for example, on the day-to-day politics of workers in the face of the production process, the working conditions, and the ways in which shop-floor workers mobilize and organize around specific goals. By linking these two aspects of collective action, the thesis proposed a complementary perspective in which the micro-level of workers' politics could be analyzed in addition to the institutional aspects of new unionism.

Given the focus on the relationship between leaders and workers, on informal shop-floor conflicts as well as formal organizations, the qualitative method seemed more appropriate than quantitative methods such as survey use. This choice was based on two main grounds. The first was the *sensitive nature* of the topic under investigation (for a detailed definition of "sensitive topics" see Lee and Renzetti 1990). The second factor in my choice of method was related to the first and referred to the nature of the answers being pursued. I would argue that it was through in-depth interviews that it became possible to overcome two types of problems. One was the need to break with the "ready made" discourse of some of the politically articulate union leaders and activists—which made it difficult for the researcher to understand substantive issues such as the underlying nature of political splits or the types of "nonexplicit" goals pursued by the leadership. In this respect, in-depth interviews with a flexible schedule allowed me to return and sometimes insist on the clarification of some points. The second problem was located on the other extreme, in interviews with people who were not articulate, not organized, and sometimes very reticent to engage in conversation about a "sensitive topic" such as union and shop-floor politics. For this group, long and open interviews allowed for the building of "trust" and "rapport" between interviewee and interviewer, as well as for the use of workers' own language and terms which in many ways make it easier to solve the communication problem.

Fieldwork was undertaken among a group of steelworkers at the National Steel Company in Rio de Janeiro, Brazil. This group was selected for the case study on the grounds that they constituted a "critical case" of the "new unionist" union.[10] Although the plant in question had been in operation since 1946, it was only after the victory of the union opposition in 1984 that the first strike among its manual work force took place. Since then, there have been 10 strikes at the plant, with ever greater radicalization expressed in actions such as plant occupations and the expulsion of management from the shop-floor by the workers. On four occasions the Brazilian army intervened to end the strikes and occupations by repressive action.

I lived in Volta Redonda, the working-class town where the National Steel Company is located, from April to July 1988 and returned to the field in January/February 1990. I carried out 72 taped interviews. Fifty-five of these interviews were with male steelworkers who either worked at the plant or were activists and union officials in the Metalworkers Union of Volta Redonda. Five were second time interviews with the same informants. The remaining 12 interviews were carried out with company management, Catholic Church leaders, steelworkers' wives engaged in community movements, a union lawyer, and union advisers.

Fifty-five interviews were obtained through the "random snowball" technique which started through two different networks: contacts in the Metalworkers' Union of Volta Redonda and contacts in the Catholic Church diocese of Volta Redonda which is the meeting place of the "Workers' Pastoral" (Pastoral Operaria) (for a detailed discussion on the "snowball technique" see Biernacki and Waldorf 1981, p. 155). The interviews were based on a set of questions which concerned the informant's work history before joining the National Steel Company, his family background in manual work, and how he got the job in the plant. I asked about his education and training, a description of present and former jobs, job routine, perception of the production process as a whole—"do you know how steel is made?"—and levels of discretion over his job. I also asked for value judgments about his work, about working in a state-owned plant, and about relations with other work mates and with management. An important set of questions were designed to find out information on shop-floor conflicts the worker had knowledge of and/or had participated in—especially the nature and dimension of the shop-floor conflicts, the protagonists involved, and the ways in which the conflicts were played out.[11]

Another set of questions referred to the informant's participation in, and views about, the union. I asked about the history of his "unionization," and would try to bring this history up to the present day. When he was not unionized, I would try to discover the reasons for that. The day-to-day union presence in the plant and the content of activist action were also explored. Questions were asked about the worker's views on the 10 strikes in the company since 1984 and about his behavior of participating or withdrawing during the strikes.

Participation in non-union associations such as Church and community gatherings, as well as political party preferences (if any) were also explored.

Finally, there was a set of specific questions for the workers who were leaders. I was interested in tracing the process of their "politicization," their affiliation to political parties and organizations, if any, as well as their overall assessment of the union government since the birth of the "Union Opposition Group." I also tried to explore their position in relation to the different workers' autonomous confederations of the time—CUT, CGT, and CGT—as well as their short-term and long-term goals as leaders. Questions were asked about the different factions inside and outside the union, and I tried to locate the leaders' own position in relation to the splits that were taking place. A further set of questions concerned the everyday and administration of the union, the decision-making process, the forms of accountability to the rank and file, and the ways in which policy priorities were drawn.

THE CODE-MAPPING OF QUALITATIVE DATA

Back in London I started the difficult and time-consuming process of transcribing all this material into the computer. I have used The Ethnograph software for the group of 60 interviews with steelworkers. The other 12 interviews were put aside, to be treated as complementary material and for cross-checking information. In the code mapping process of the 60 interviews, I created 64 different codes. As an exercise "a posteriori," after much coding, recoding, and re-reading of the numbered transcriptions, it was clear that the code mapping process had operated under an analytical system, even though this had initially been quite unconscious.

The codes had three basic levels of abstraction, or three "types of codes." The first type may be called "information codes" which are of a very concrete level and are usually, but not necessarily, segments of text which refer to dates of events, names of people and places, and quantities.

The second type of code was based on the informants' categories, perceptions, and beliefs. An example of such a "category code" includes "*peao*" which is a name which all workers identify themselves with and which unites the majority of workers. Every manual worker in the plant was a "*peao.*" By contrast, only some workers were "professionals" and this based the differentiation among all "*peoes.*" The third group of categories might be called "analytical"—they result from the researcher's perceptions of links that are not self-evident and constitute an instance of synthesis. Taking the above example further, "identity" and "differentiation" are analytical codes derived from "*peao*" and "professional." Another example of "analytical codes" are the three "political types" devised by the researcher and which are suggested to exist in other "new unionist" settings in Brazil. They are the "Trade Union Paternalist," the "Radical Reformist," and the "Revolutionary."

It is worth noting that in my experience, the types of codes attached to segments of text changed as the analysis developed. Some "information codes," for example, were later turned into "categorial" or "analytical" codes, in an interchangeable process. For example, a comprehensive account by an informant of the production process of steel might be read initially as an "information code." However, it can also be read as structured knowledge about the production process and an expressive indicator of the worker's skill level. In this case the same segment of text which was coded as an "information code" would have turned into a "categorial code" reflecting the researcher's new insight over the same textual data.

As pointed out earlier, the process of coding is a first, and very important stage of analysis, which must be followed by a second stage, the actual searching of codes. In the "search process" the researcher can test the richness of an insight, the levels of recurrence of patterns, the context in which these patterns vary, and the remaining analytical syntheses which social scientists should offer.

In the searching process the "face-sheet" feature offered in The Ethnograph allows the researcher to explore variations in the data through clearly delineated variables. As Seidel et al. (1988, pp. 14-21) have pointed out, face-sheets allow the researcher to add an additional dimension to the analysis of the data, complementary to the codes that have been used to define segments of text.

In order to use face-sheets in the search it is first necessary to create a template—that is, a list of the names of the variables and details about whether the variable is numerical or textual. After the template is created, one can create a face-sheet for each of the data files. This means that the program will ask the researcher to "answer" the specific values of each variable, for each data file (Seidel et al. 1988, pp. 15-21). Once this is done, up to six variables can be used during the "search a code procedure" for *selective searches*, enhancing the analytical possibilities of the data.

Some observers may see in the face-sheets a danger of the "numericization" of qualitative data. I would argue, first, that as the variables can be either numbers or text, this danger does not exist. Second, I tend to agree with Bulmer (1979, p. 673) when he states that to rule out measurement in principle in qualitative research is an error. I suggest that different forms of measurement can complement the analysis of qualitative data.

In my research I have used face-sheets with "variables." These included: age, number of years at school, title of last job, department at the plant, stage of the production line which the job is linked to, if unionized, preference of vote in last union election, if has used the Brazilian labor courts to sort out grievances with management, how many times and when, vote in last national elections, political party affiliation (if any), among others.

A simple example of a selective search using face-sheet variables would be to search for all instances of segments coded as *"union participation," with the face-sheet variable for age*, and see to what extent the steelworkers' generation can help to explain higher levels militancy.

The findings of the case study in the thesis suggested that the contribution of the new union movement was specially significant in the politicized use of the CIPA (*Comissao Interna de Prevencao de Acidentes*—Internal Committee for the Prevention of Accidents) and in the innovative use of the Labor Courts. The significance of these dimensions was that they involved an attempt to expand workers' rights as well as to create new basis under which their rights are granted. On the other hand, the case study suggested that the internal dynamics of the "new union" movement still have elements which may be characterized as non-democratic, and that this generated a new set of problems and dilemmas for organized labor in Brazil during the 1990s.

This brief description has, I hope, demonstrated the immense possibilities opened up by the use of a computer program where qualitative data is treated appropriately. The Ethnograph program has offered me analytical possibilities which would have been extremely difficult (and some altogether impossible), if the manual handling of 60 lengthy interviews was used.

CONCLUSION

This paper illustrated the use of a particular software package—The Ethnograph—for the analysis of qualitative data in a sociological investigation. Qualitative researchers can benefit greatly from specially designed computer software such as The Ethnograph since it allows for the adequate treatment of non-numerical data.

In my view, the use of computers for this type of analysis constitutes not only a change of degree in the sense that the researcher can penetrate deeper into his material because he or she is freed from the mechanical aspect of analysis, but also a change of kind. The argument I wish to make is that the computer not only increases the speed, efficiency, and capacity of analysis— it also provides new ways of looking at data, by helping the user to work simultaneously, with a variety of data. Finally it is possible to suggest that this new qualitative software will allow for greater comparative exercises between monographs and case studies since the classification and retrieval of data can be done with greater rigor and ease.

Having set out the positive side of the "computer revolution" for qualitative researchers, it seems appropriate to outline the problems inherent in this new trend.

The first problem refers to the sociological bias of the creator of the software and his or her way of working, neither of which are self-evident to the user. In Seidel's software for example, the researcher is deliberately invited to leave the computer for the code mapping process and must "code" segments on a blank screen, detached from the original transcripts. The researcher can also quantify certain aspects of his or her data through the face-sheet and frequency features. All these features constitute options that were taken while the software was being created and reflect the bias and the authors' way of working. I think that this is true for all software packages but even more so for the "expert-systems," which aspire to generate some level of interpretation and inference of data.

One possible problem with "expert-systems" is the imposition by computer scientists of their own "rational models" on to sociology, without these being completely intelligible to the discipline. This is due to the fact that "expert-systems" are based on underlying "rationales" which are external to sociological paradigms. Concepts such as "consistency," "inconsistency," and "contradictions" can have very different meanings for a sociologist and a computer scientist. The way out of this problem seems to be the accessibility of comprehensive information about the different software available and a proper debate within the social science community about their comparative benefits.

A second problem is the risk of a certain degree of "computer domination." By this I mean an almost caricatured situation of risk in which the increasing use of qualitative software by social scientists might become a "fashionable vogue" whereby computer-assisted analysis gain immediate legitimization, against what could be seen as "old-fashioned and traditional" manual analysis. I would like to argue in favor of a pluralistic approach which legitimizes the researcher's decision to use or not to use computer software programs, as well as the need for comprehensive information, so that the researcher can choose the most suitable software package for his or her research. In this pluralistic position, standards are set in accordance with the criterion of rigor and quality, for as Frantzich and Purtkitt (1987, p. 501) have stated, the sign of a good researcher is knowing when to reach for which tool.

NOTES

1. This paper is a revised version of a paper presented to the International Sociological Association and prized by ISA in the "young sociologists" competition. ISA, Madrid, 1990.

2. I have greatly benefited from participating in two challenging conferences on "Qualitative Knowledge and Computing." The first, was held at the University of Surrey, in July 1989. It was organized by Dr. R Lee and Dr. N. Fielding. The second took place October 1992 in Bremen and was organized by Udo kelle. In both conferences, qualitative researchers and computer scientists from Europe, the United States, Brazil, and Australia debated and evaluated this new trend.

3. Mainframe refers to large, central computers developed in the 1950s and 1960s. It is also a general term for a multi-user computer designed to meet the computing needs of a large organization as opposed to personal computers of more limited use (QUE's Computer User's Dictionary 1990, p. 285).

4. Although the microcomputer has been commercially available since the early 1970s, its expanded use by social scientists is a more recent phenomenon. In the United States, for example, a survey conducted by the American Council of Learned Societies found that 95 percent of scholars had access to a computer in 1985, as compared with only 2 percent in 1980 (Hinze 1987, p. 440).

5. It is important to note that there is opposition to further computerization in the social sciences, as computers are held responsible for the over-numericization of social science research (Sproull and Sproull 1982, p. 288). This reaction is difficult to trace and comment upon but Frantzich and Purkitt (1987, p. 486) has suggested that there tends to be a generational aspect in the reaction whereby senior academics are more reluctant to the computer penetration than their students.

6. Two examples of this trend include a knowledge-based program called "N-ACT" which uses Goffman's dramatic model to analyze social integration, designed by Brent (1986) and an unfinished program by Finkelstein (1989) which proposes to "describe social behaviour and theories about social behaviour and make verifiable predictions from descriptions," applied to an ethnography of an urban Punjabi community in Pakistan. The first project is linked to the University of Missouri. The second is a co-research project between the University of Kent and Imperial College, London.

7. The Ethnograph software runs on IBM-PCs, XTs, ATs, and compatibles. It requires at least 256k of memory. Two floppy disk drives or one floppy disk drive and a hard disk are required to run the program.

8. In The Ethnograph "overlapping segments" are coded segments that share one or more lines of the data file. "Nested segments" are coded segments that are completely contained within a larger coded segment (Seidel et al. 1988, pp. 7-12.

9. For the purpose of this paper I am greatly simplifying the debate. The greater militancy of the "new unionist" movement is defined by its greater propensity to strike, in the forms of struggle it chooses, by the politicized use of legal channels, and by the introduction of issues which question the organization of production.

The "new unionist" unions are defined as more representative of their rank and file because they allow for the emergence of new protagonists as union leaders, they allow for and encouraged workplace representation, they have attempted to broaden the basis of participation, and have allowed for systematic union elections.

This was how the literature available defined and characterized the movement (see Alvaro Moises 1982; Humphrey 1980, 1982; Tavares de Almeida 1983; Keck 1989; and Moreira Alves 1988 among others).

10. By critical case is meant an empirical situation which meets all the conditions for the testing of a theory, whether it confirms, challenges, or extends that theory (see Yin 1989, p. 47).

11. Interviews were carried out in the workers' homes, at the Union, and diocese offices. The interviews were semi-structured—I had an initial set of questions which I wanted to cover during the interview, but I was willing to change this if the informant brought a different set of interests and priorities.

The interview schedule was used much more as a checklist of issues on which I wanted the informants to comment than as a closed-type questionnaire.

REFERENCES

Alvaro Moises, J.

1982 "What is the Strategy of the 'New Syndicalism'?" In *Latin American Perspective* 35(9)(4)(fall).

Biernacki, P., and D. Waldorf

1981 "Snowball Sampling. Problems and Techniques of Chain Referral Sampling." *Sociological Methods and Research* 10(2)(November).

Brent, E.E.

1986 "Knowledge-Based Systems: A Qualitative Formalism." In *Qualitative Sociology* 9(3)(fall).

Bulmer, M.

1979 "Concepts in the Analysis of Qualitative Data." *Sociological Review* 27(4).

Burawoy, M.

1987 *The Politics of Production*. London: Verso Press (1st ed. 1985).

Evans, M., and R. Bernard

1983 "New Microcomputer Techniques for Anthropologists." *Human Organization* 42(2)(summer).

Fielding, N., and R. Lee (Eds).

1991 *Using Commuters in Qualitative Research*. London: Sage.

Fielding, N.

1993 *Social Research Update*. University of Surrey. March.

Finkelstein, A.

1989 "A Case Study in Social Knowledge Representation." Conference on Qualitative Knowledge and Computing. Survey (mimeo).

Frantzich, S., and H. Purkitt
1987 "Computers in Political Science." *Social Science Microcomputer Review* 5(4)(winter).

Gerson, E.
1986 "Computing in Qualitative Sociology: An Approach to Structures Text." *Qualitative Sociology* 9(2)(summer).

Halfpenny, P.
1979 "Analysis of Qualitative Data." *Sociological Review*27(4).

Hinze, K.
1987 "Computing in Sociology: Bringing Back the Balance." *Social Science Microcomputer Review* 5(4)(winter).

Hudson, R., and N. Hudson
1986 "Computers for Anthropological Fieldwork." *Current Anthropology* 27(5)(December).

Humphrey, J.
1980 "As Raizes e os Desafios do 'Novo Sindicalismo,' da Industria Automobilistica." *Estudos CEBRAP* 26.

Humphrey, J.
1982 *Capitalist Control and Workers' Struggle in the Brazilian Auto Industry*. Princeton, NJ: Princeton University Press.

Keck, M.
1989 "New Unionism in the Brazilian Transition." In *Democratizing Brazil: Problems of Transition and Consolidation*, edited by A. Stephan. Oxford: Oxford University Press.

Lee, R., and C. Renzetti
1990 "The Problems of Researching Sensitive Topics." In *American Behavioural Scientist* 33(5)(May-June).

Mangabeira, W.
1991 *Union Politics and Workplace Militancy: A Case Study of Brazilian Steelworkers in the 1980s*. London School of Economics and Political Science, University of London.

Mangabeira, W.
1993 *Dilemas do "Novo Sindicalismo." Democracia e Politica em Volta Redonda*. Rio de Janeiro: Relume Dumara.

Michels, R.
1959 *Political Parties*. New York: Dover Publications. (First edition 1915).

Moreira Alves, M.
1988 "Trade Unions in Brazil. A Search for Autonomy and Organization." In *Labour Autonomy and the State in Latin America*, edited by E. Epstein. London: Unwin Hyman.

Patton, P., and R. Holoien
1981 *Computing in the Humanities*. Hampshire: Gower Publishing.

Rahtz, S. (Ed).
1987 *Information Technology in the Humanities: Tools, Techniques and Applications*. New York: Halsted Press.

Seidel, S., R. Kjolseth, and E. Seymour
1988 *The Ethnograph. Software Manual.* Littleton, CO: Qualis Research Associates. (First version 1985).

Sproull, L., and R. Sproull
1982 "Managing and Analyzing Behavioural Records: Explorations in Non-Numeric Data Analysis." *Human Organization* 41(4)(winter).

Tavares de Almeida, M.H.
1983 "Novas Demandas, Novos Direitos: Experiencias do Sindicalismo Paulista das Ultimas Decadas." *DADOS* 26(3).

Tesch, R.
1990 *Qualitative Research: Analylsis Types and Software Tools.* London: Falmer Press.

Yin, R.
1989 *Case Study Research and Design Methods.* London: Sage Publications.

FINDING A "ROLE" FOR THE ETHNOGRAPH IN THE ANALYSIS OF QUALITATIVE DATA

Derrick Armstrong

INTRODUCTION

The procedures and techniques used by qualitative researchers when analyzing their data are shrouded in an enduring mystique. One stage removed from the analysis of actual data there have been a number of well known accounts of the principles underpinning data analysis which have had considerable influence on the task that researchers perceive themselves to be doing when they are analyzing data. In particular "analytic induction" (Robinson 1951) and "grounded theory" (Glaser and Strauss 1967) are frequently invoked. Burgess (1984) has commented upon the importance of evaluating the processes involved in the analysis of data and the

Studies in Qualitative Methodology, Volume 5, pages 63-79.

ISBN: 1-55938-902-8.

writing up of research reports but, as he has commented elsewhere (Burgess 1992), although qualitative researchers are generally good at providing detailed accounts of their data collection procedures they are rarely explicit about the procedures they use to analyze this data:

> there are few accounts of the way in which these processes actually occur as opposed to the way they are supposed to occur (Burgess 1992, p. 2).

When I started out on my first major research project (Armstrong 1993) I remember being gripped by that combination of enthusiasm and naiveté that is such a wonderfully powerful stimulant for reinventing the wheel. This naiveté was gradually stripped away by my growing awareness of the intractability of some of the problems with which more experienced researchers had been engaged over a long period of time. Nevertheless, I soon realized that when it comes to explaining what they do when analyzing their data social scientists tend to draw the sort of large-scale maps of the world that are not very useful for traversing mountain ridges.

Some researchers have referred to the practical processes of "cut and paste" they have used for managing their data and exploring categories of analysis. However, the development of modem computer technologies have opened up possibilities for using more efficient and systematic techniques in the analysis of qualitative data. On the other hand the use of computers in qualitative data analysis can have disadvantages as well as advantages. For instance, problems can stem from the possibilities open to the researcher for generating larger and larger numbers of categories without anything necessarily being added to a theoretical understanding of the issues being investigated. In other words, with this technology the very ease of operation can create conditions under which theory generation becomes subsumed under a welter of empirical classification.

My own introduction to the use of computers for data analysis came with the decision to use The Ethnograph (Seidel et al. 1988) for analyzing data collected during research for my Ph.D. Prior to this I had no experience of using computer-based data analysis packages but I was encouraged by the enthusiasm of colleagues in the department who had recently started to experiment with The Ethnograph in their research. I was also influenced by the fact that the package provided a framework of practical guidelines for the analysis of data, something which was noticeably absent from the texts which up to that time I had been reading.

In this paper I want to describe my experiences of working with the Ethnograph, the ways in which this assisted the process of data analysis, but also to identify some of the difficulties I encountered and how these eventually led to a more limited role for the Ethnograph than I had first anticipated.

THE RESEARCH

My research was undertaken as part of a wider European and Social Research Council-funded study of participant perspectives on the assessment of children's special educational needs under the 1981 Education Act where those needs were initially identified by teachers, and in some cases by parents, as arising because of emotional and behavioral difficulties (Galloway et al. 1994). I was particularly interested in the experiences children and their parents had of the assessment process, their contributions to that process and the ways in which client and professional identities were constructed during the process of assessment. There were both theoretical and practical reasons for focusing on emotional and behavioral difficulties. There is evidence that increasing numbers of children are being excluded from their mainstream schools because their teachers perceive their behavior to be a serious impediment to the effective classroom learning of all children (Pyke 1992). Second, there is widespread uncertainty over the meaning of such terms as "emotional and behavioral difficulties," "maladjustment," and "behavioral disorder." The criteria used by teachers and other professionals to identify these children are rarely made explicit and these terms may actually be applied to children whose behavior is unacceptable to the personal values of particular teachers in specific contexts. Yet there is extensive evidence pointing to differences in the behavior of children in different situations. Children do not always behave in the same way with all teachers, nor do teachers agree on the behaviors they regard as unacceptable. Despite this, professionals are more likely to locate the origin of difficult behavior in the child's home background than with any other group of children with special educational needs (Moses and Croll 1987). In these circumstances, the different perspectives on the child's behavior held by parents, professionals, and children are likely to have important implications for the outcome of any subsequent assessment. In the absence of "objective" criteria the needs of children may be negotiated within a context of differing interests, making the power of participants vis-à-vis each other an major factor influencing both how and what decisions are made during the assessment.

In order to examine the interactions between participants in the assessment process and to explore how their perspectives on emotional and behavioral difficulties might be developed during the course of the assessment itself it was decided to undertake a case study analysis of the assessment of children in three local education authorities. In all, 29 children took part in this part of the study. Whenever possible, observations were made of interviews related to each child's assessment, for example between educational psychologists and parents, and between psychologists and children. Examinations of children by clinical medical officers were also attended and detailed discussions of each case were held with head and class teachers. Subsequently each participant in the study was interviewed separately to elicit and discuss their perceptions of the purpose of each stage of the assessment together with their beliefs about what had been achieved. Table 1 summarizes the range of observations and interviews that were conducted during the course of the research.

In addition to the 29 children participating in the case study component of the research, 18 more children, drawn from an off-site behavioral unit for primary-age children and two residential special schools for secondary-age pupils were interviewed about their experiences and beliefs about the assessment process.

Table 1. Research Observations and Interviews

Assessment Interviews Observed		*Researcher's Interviews with Participants*	
Psychologists' interviews with children	18	Parents	51
Psychologists' interviews with parents	24	Children	33
Psychologists' interviews with teachers	12	Psychologists	60
Welfare officers' interviews with parents	6	Clinical medical officers	20
Case conferences	13	Teachers (mainstream)	46
Statutory medical examinations	12	Teachers (special school)	14
Court hearings	2	Social workers	7
Classroom observations by psychologists	6	Education welfare officers	5
		Psychiatrists	1
		Administrators/LEA advisers	4

DO COMPUTERS REALLY DO ALL THIS? SOME EARLY THOUGHTS ON GROUNDED THEORY AND THE SYSTEMATIC ANALYSIS OF DATA

Computers have become such an important tool in my daily work, it comes as something of a shock now when I remember that before 1989 I had never used a computer in my work at all. When at the outset of the project, the university decided to provide a machine for my use I remember sitting in front of the screen wondering whether by switching it on I might initiate an uncontrollable series of events which would result in its destruction. Later, when I had managed to decipher the manual sufficiently to realize that it was probably safe to do so, the computer became a wonderful toy, although I remained unsure as to whether I was actually saving working time by using it or whether I was simply adding the duties of a secretary to my own job description. My fascination with what could be done on the computer was endless but one of my most powerful memories of those early days was that of my disappointment when I realized that the "language choice" option on my word processing package did not allow me to instantly translate from English into French at the push of a button. Naive as this might sound, my expectations of The Ethnograph were to some extent analogous.

Once I had made the decision to use The Ethnograph, rather than finding myself liberated, I felt quite disabled. I was faced with a number of delays and inconveniences that seemed to prevent me from coming to grips with the analysis of my ever growing collection of interview transcripts and observation schedules. I had to send off to the United States for a copy of the program and when a copy eventually did arrive (the first one that was sent was lost en route) I discovered that I would have to reformat all my existing word processing files to enable their conversion into Ethnograph files. These delays were frustrating but they did not in themselves prevent me from engaging in the activity of data analysis. Throughout the project I had been carrying out an analysis of my data by way of the ideas generated from observing and talking to participants in the assessment process and from my reading of transcripts. The problem was that this did not seem very systematic to me while now, with The Ethnograph, I would have the opportunity to use a computer to analyze my data. So in my own mind I was unable to analyze my data properly until The Ethnograph was up and running. This sense of dependency was not very helpful, inhibiting my understanding both of my data and of what I was doing as a researcher. Captivated by the prospect of systematic analysis I began to devalue my initial ideas about the data as impressionistic and "unscientific," only to discover, when the software finally did arrive, that these impressionistic ideas were not suddenly replaced by a new, more scientific, understanding. In fact it was the ideas I had developed at a much earlier point that gave me some sort of handle on the data and became the springboard for the more systematic analyses I started to work on with The Ethnograph.

The mechanical difficulties in organizing a large qualitative data base in such a way that allows the flexible manipulation and exploration of a developing category system is no easy task. Not only does systematic analysis depend upon the organization of a complex set of categories it is also important that the nature of these categories can be explored and theoretically developed across the data set. This involves far more than simply retrieving examples of those categories from the data. However, although the goal of systematic analysis appears to be a worthy one it is far from clear what this actually means. Like many qualitative researchers, I had been attracted to the method of "grounded theory" developed by

Glaser and Strauss (1967). These authors describe their approach to data analysis as offering a way of "generating theory from data" but more than that they go on to argue that

> concepts not only come from the data, but are systematically worked out in relation to the data in the course of the research (p. 6).

Glaser and Strauss are at pains to distinguish their method from what they consider to be the limitations of "analytic induction." The standard-critique of inductive method, of course, is that explanations based upon this method can never achieve the status of proof while there are possible cases that might now or in the future provide a disproof (Popper 1959). Whereas inductive methodologies aim to prove or disprove hypotheses, grounded theory is concerned with generating theory through the "saturation" of categories. The "saturation" of categories does not involve testing a hypothesis on every *possible* case to which the hypothesis would apply. Rather, "saturation" is a theoretical concept which describes a situation in which new data no longer contributes to the development of the properties of the category.

According to Glaser and Strauss, both substantive and formal theory (with the former necessarily preceding the latter) develop out of the generalized relations which may be observed between categories. Formal theory, as distinct from substantive theory which is linked specifically to particular data sets, involves a further stage of theory generation whereby an abstraction from comparative data sets is made and theorized to more general situations. It is the role of theory to provide a framework for understanding. The predictive capacity of theory is not precluded, but the role of prediction is linked to theory generation rather than theory testing. This distinction is quite crucial.

The idea that categories are grounded in data and that theory is generated from categories is not unproblematic. In the past there has often been a gap between the methodological sophistication that can be attributed to the analytical procedures of grounded theory and the inadequacy of the tools available to qualitative researchers for manipulating their data. Very often this has led to an idealized and sanitized representation of grounded theory, one that is not always recognizable to those engaged in "real" research. In part, I believe, this is one reason why there is so little evidence of how these procedures are used, despite the commitment so many researchers express toward them. In consequence, statements about the use of these procedures may say more about the mores and expectations of the academic community than anything about the uses of systematic methods of data analysis.

The initial appeal of The Ethnograph for me lay in the degree of technical sophistication it offered for manipulating data, allowing systematic exploration of patterns and themes occurring within that data. This was not simply about the speed at which information could be processed; it was more about the ease of movement around the data and the emerging system of codes and the comprehensive way in which these movements could be monitored. Another advantage of this program was that a high level of technical skill was not required in order to carry out quite complex data searches. Moreover, the procedures for organizing data had been developed through use on real-life projects and their clarity and lack of rigidity reflected their origins in grounded theory. The program had been developed on the basis of methodological principles and reflection and therefore was aimed at facilitating procedures that researchers already used in their analysis rather than redefining those procedures to fit what could be done using computer technology. As I became more familiar with The Ethnograph it soon became very clear that this was one of its main strengths but it also became clear that it was only an aid to analysis.

USING THE ETHNOGRAPH: OPPORTUNITIES AND LIMITATIONS

In principle, The Ethnograph claims to treat data in broadly the same way as would be the case if it were analyzed by hand. Thus, the role of the computer is that of an information processing system which increases the speed at which data can be processed, enabling the easy retrieval of data structured according to a complex, yet flexible, set of user-defined data codes. Data is first entered into the word processor before being imported by The Ethnograph which then numbers each data line. It is in this numbered format that the main operation of data analysis takes place. This analysis (as distinct from the mundane operation of data processing based on the analysis carried out by the researcher) is undertaken by the researcher who codes the paper copy of each file. Once this print-out has been coded by hand these codes are entered into the computer referenced against line numbers in the data file. These coded files can be proofread and edited, including modifications to the entire coding system by adding and deleting codes or changing the boundaries of coded segments. The capacity to accept detailed modification of the coding system at any stage during the analysis is indeed a feature of the program which allows for the evolution of the coding system as the researcher's understanding of the data develops or new data is collected. Segments of data may be simultaneously coded in different ways allowing different interpretations to be worked through as well as allowing an exploration of the conceptual connections between different parts of the data.

My naiveté about The Ethnograph was not so great that I believed all I needed to do was enter my data and the program would do the rest but there was a sense in which I believed that once I had identified the categories I wanted to use the computer would carry out the analysis and not me. There was nothing in The Ethnograph program that directly encouraged this. Indeed the manual clearly stated:

> In developing THE ETHNOGRAPH it was important for us to distinguish conceptually between the interpretive (or thinking) parts of the work, and the mechanical parts of qualitative data analysis. What troubled us was the idea that our computer program would be misperceived as able to take over some of the thinking parts of the analytic process. If that were the case it would be likely to unduly control the analytic process. This was something we did not (and do not) want to happen (Seidel et al. 1988, pp. 1-3).

Nonetheless, this distinction between the mechanical and thinking parts of data analysis is not, as I found out, quite so straightforward. The emphasis that The Ethnograph places on the categorization of data segments can be misleading insofar as it encourages a belief in categorization as the principal objective of analysis rather than simply as one stage in the analysis. More than that, if The Ethnograph is seen as a complete system for the analysis of data rather than as a tool contributing to that process, then the mechanical process of coding and comparing data segments may encourage an over-emphasis upon those aspects of the data which are accessible for retrieval by The Ethnograph at the expense of others that may be less so. In order to maximize the effectiveness of The Ethnograph it is important to understand just what it does and, therefore its limitations. Failing this, the mechanical process may influence the nature of the analysis. For instance, I found that The Ethnograph lent itself very well to identifying instances of particular themes across cases. This was a feature of the program which was of considerable value because it helped in really getting to know the data well and also because it helped me to present a detailed description of its features. On the other hand, I found it less helpful when it came to the analysis of particular cases. In part this was to do with the way I used cases in this research. In focusing upon particular cases I was more concerned with analyzing why certain relationships occurred than with simply identifying the features of the case. In other words, coding segments of data was less important than the activity of theorizing. I was using individual cases to theorize on the basis of categories developed at an earlier stage of the analysis.

In reporting my own research I felt it was important to map out the broad features of the database I was using. To this end The Ethnograph proved to be a valuable tool. Once the data had been coded it was relatively easy to retrieve material in a form that made this preliminary descriptive account quite straightforward. The general framework for this reflected questions I had at the outset of the research. For instance, I wanted to identify how the accounts of participants in the assessment process might differ according to their role as teacher, psychologist, doctor, parent, child, and so forth. I also wanted to know something about the expectations different participants had of the assessment at its outset and how those expectations had been fulfilled or modified as the assessment proceeded. The Ethnograph proved itself well suited to collating information that was useful in describing these and many other features of the database. More than this it was helpful in providing some preliminary analysis of a range of different perspectives held by participants with similar as well as different roles. Thus, I was able to see that accounts of the purpose of the assessment given by parents in my sample fell into two broad and to some extent overlapping categories. In 10 cases parents saw the purpose as predominantly concerned with identifying what was wrong with the child. In these accounts children's needs were represented in terms of a medical or treatment model. In 14 cases parents adopted a conflict model of the assessment in which these procedures were seen as being initiated to legitimize the views of teachers against those of parents. These preliminary analyses using The Ethnograph were useful insofar as they helped me to explore the composition and structure of my data and to provide a full description of the data that I had collected. Offering a full description of the database to the reader of qualitative research is something that I believe to be important.

The sort of evidence provided by a full description of the database does not in itself provide a sufficient basis for generalization beyond that data but it does permit the researcher to say something about the "relevance" of the data. It does so by providing other researchers and practitioners the opportunity to evaluate the extent to which the data is typical or atypical in the light of their own research and/or experience. To some extent this process of description involves quantifying the data and The Ethnograph is very useful in this respect because it enables the researcher to quickly locate, collate, and contrast coded segments. However, in carrying out this sort of analysis care is needed so as not to be misled into over-emphasizing the explanatory power of quantification based on a very small sample of cases. Knowing that a particular construct occurred within 28 of the 29 cases is interesting and does, as Hammersley (1992) has argued, make a stronger case for generalizability than would have been the case if it had occurred in only one case. It should be noted as well that the level of incidence only illuminates a theme that is being analyzed, it does not in itself constitute the analysis. The Ethnograph is particularly useful for identifying illustrative material but a large amount of analysis remains to be done if illustrative material is to be used analytically. With research such as my own, the really interesting part of the analysis came, alter the relevance of the data had been established, with the detailed consideration of individual cases. What was important here was how particular processes operated in specific cases. In this respect I found The Ethnograph to be less useful.

Of the codes I used in this study one was concerned with the perceptions different participants had of the role of educational psychologists while a second sought to identify how those psychologists understood their own role in assessments of special educational needs. Analysis of these codes using The Ethnograph revealed that psychologists tended to adopt different roles at different times during the assessment. In some cases there was evidence of psychologists changing their role at different points in their interviews with parents and with teachers. The roles adopted by psychologists included those of adviser, advocate, diagnostician, administrator, and so forth. In addition, analysis of observation schedules and interviews with other participants, again using The Ethnograph for processing codes and retrieving data, revealed that parents, teachers, Local Education Authority officers, and, to a much lesser extent, children all believed themselves to be clients of the psychologist (though not necessarily simultaneously or at all stages of the assessment) with legitimate expectations of the service that the psychologist was, or ought to be, providing for them. This was an interesting finding on the basis of which it was possible to say something about the contradictions within the role of the educational psychologist and how these contradictions might undermine the independence of psychologists' contributions to these assessments. However, this finding did not explain how competition between these legitimate expectations influenced the way psychologists perceived their roles and how they attempted to reconcile or otherwise deal with contradictory expectations in their practice.

In order to further the analysis of these themes it was necessary to do more than retrieve and compare coded segments from different cases in the database. What was needed was a close analysis of how these themes developed and operated in particular cases. To do this I needed to consider cases holistically so that I could analytically reconstruct them to show how interactions between various participants, including those like the LEA who were not involved in face-to-face negotiations, led to particular outcomes. This part of the analysis is essentially inferential rather than descriptive and as such it represents an interpretation of the case supported by evidence. The analysis of the assessment of Ben, one of the children in the study, may illustrate this.

Ben had attended an off-site unit for children with behavioral difficulties since he was 7 years old. Now that Ben was 11 years old his parents wanted him to be integrated into a mainstream primary school before reaching secondary school age. In agreeing to an assessment of his special educational needs they relied upon the educational psychologist to help achieve this goal. In other words, they expected an advocacy model of intervention. The parents' objectives were supported by the psychologist who negotiated quite forcefully with the LEA to secure Ben's reintegration into mainstream schooling. A primary school was identified that was willing to accept Ben but only on the condition that additional resources would be made available by the LEA to support this. The LEA, however, was unwilling to provide these resources on the grounds that if resources "so in excess of the normal provision in a mainstream school are required to make reintegration feasible, then the child is not yet ready for reintegration." From this point onward the psychologist's advocacy on behalf of the parents came into conflict with the school's expectation of him as a resource manager (based on their belief that they were the psychologist's client) and with the LEA's expectations of him as a consultant providing independent advice (based on a belief that they as the psychologist's employers were his principal clients). Potentially the differing expectations of each of these clients could bring the psychologist into conflict with them all. Conflict with the LEA was possible if he chose to use the assessment procedures as a way of obtaining additional resources which the LEA had previously refused to make available. Conflict with parents occurred when the latter became suspicious of the psychologist as an LEA officer when he would not and could not guarantee what the outcome would be. Conflict with the school arose when the head teacher became unhappy with the psychologist's failure to deliver the resources that were perceived to be necessary by the staff at the school. Thus the psychologist's loyalties were divided as he became the focus of conflict between his clients.

In a discussion of qualitative methodology Strauss (1988) argued that researchers cannot simply discover grounded theory but rather that they are participants in its development. This suggests that grounded theory is primarily concerned with opening up ways of thinking about data. It is not a set of prescriptive rules which, if followed to the letter, will lead the researcher to the "truth." It rather provides a set of guidelines for assisting the researcher to think in creative ways about the interpretation of data while also subjecting the researcher's developing perspective to scrutiny by reference to the data.

The analysis of data involves a dialectic between the researcher and the data, a dialectic in which meanings are constructed and not simply found. The coding of data is itself part of this interpretative process and caution is needed to avoid the pitfall of believing that systematic analysis is synonymous with gaining access to an objective truth. The systematic analysis that is facilitated by The Ethnograph is, nonetheless important in that it opens up possibilities for exploring data in ways which may lead to more plausible and authentic stories being told. In this respect qualitative research is analogous with the historical research in which authenticity and validity are the key criteria of evaluation. The nature of the qualitative research activity in the social sciences, however, differs from that of history because the researcher is a part of the setting that is being researched (either as a participant or as an observer).

In recording interactions, whether these are the outcomes of interviews or of observation, there is a danger of over-emphasizing the verbal. Such a lot of what goes on in these interactions, however, is non-verbal. It is possible to use The Ethnograph for analyzing non-verbal data if these are represented in the form of research notes yet this may be problematic insofar as the format of recording best suited to the Ethnograph may not adequately represent the nature of the interactions taking place. For instance, in recording observations, seating plans or sociometric maps may be a more appropriate unit of analysis than Ethno-compatible notes. Of course, this may merely lead one to conclude that the analysis of transcripts using the Ethnograph should not dominate the process of analysis at the expense of other ways equally useful to recording and looking at data. However, there is, I believe, a more important reservation that needs to be voiced in respect to the limitations of The Ethnograph.

The observer of social interaction and participants in those interactions (e.g., interviewers) are continually engaged in a social process of constructing frameworks within which meanings are represented. These frameworks are by their nature implicit in the interaction itself and may become an important contextualizing factor in any subsequent analyses. The identification of what constitutes data, the interpretation of that data, and the generation and development of theory to account for data is not simply the outcome of a systematic analysis of data segments but is also based upon the presentation of a plausible account or story about the world. Such accounts are not only informed by the data they explain and the data they do not explain, but also by interactions taking place during the observation or within the interview which themselves provide a context for interpreting data which has been reproduced in the form of transcripts.

WAS IT WORTH IT?

By the end of my research, The Ethnograph had come to provide, for me, just one, albeit very important, window on my data. Increasingly, I found myself working with the numbered print outs to explore individual case studies rather than with the comparison of decontextualized coded segments across cases. Ironically, the most significant way in which The Ethnograph contributed to this analysis was in its requirement of a maximum line length of 40 characters. This ensured that there was a half-page right-hand margin that created a simple but highly effective thinking space on the page. In the earlier stages of the analysis, however, I had found The Ethnograph to be a valuable device for getting to know the quantitative boundaries of the data. Partly, this was helpful because it enabled me to make a case for the relevance of the data. In addition, although there are limitations to the conclusions that can be drawn from this quantitative dimension of the analysis, it did enable the sort of systematic analysis that was useful in the preliminary stages for suggesting relationships which I was later to explore in more detail through the medium of case analysis.

ACKNOWLEDGMENTS

This article arises out of a research project on the "Identification of Emotional and Behavioural Difficulties: Participant Perspectives," directed by Professor David Galloway and Professor Sally Tomlinson and funded by the Economic and Social Research Council, Research Grant No. R 000 23 1393. The support of the Research Council is gratefully acknowledged.

REFERENCES

Armstrong, D.
1993 *Conflicting Perspectives on the Assessment of Emotional and Behavioural Difficulties: Children Parents and Professionals.* Unpublished Ph.D. thesis, Department of Educational Research, Lancaster University.

Burgess, R.G.
1984 *In the Field: An Introduction to Field Research.* London: George Allen and Unwin.

Burgess, R.G.
1992 "Linking Design and Analysis in Ethnographic Studies." Paper presented to the British Educational Research Association Annual Conference, Stirling.

Galloway, D., D. Armstrong, and S. Tomlinson
1994 *The Assessment of Special Educational Needs: Whose Problem?* London: Longman.

Glaser, B., and A. Strauss
1967 *The Discovery of Grounded Theory: Strategies for Qualitative Research.* Chicago: Aldine.

Hammersley, M.
1992 *What's Wrong with Ethnography?* London: Routledge.

Moses, D., and P. Croll
1987 "Parents as Partners or Problems?" *Disability, Handicap and Society* 2: 75-84.
Popper, K.
1959 *The Logic of Scientific Discovery*. London: Hutchinson.
Pyke, N.
1992 "Into the Exclusion Zone." *Times Educational Supplement* (June, 26) p. 14.
Robinson, W.S.
1951 "The Logical Structure of Analytic Induction." *American Sociological Review* 16: 812-818.
Seidel, J., R. Kjolseth, and E. Seymour
1988 *The Ethnograph*. Littleton, CO: Qualis Research Associates.
Strauss, A.
1988 "Methods and Ethics—Teaching Qualitative Research Methods Courses: A Conversation with Anselm Strauss." *International Journal of Qualitative Studies in Education* 1: 91-100.

THE DATA, THE TEAM, AND THE ETHNOGRAPH

Annemarie Sprokkereef, Emma Lakin,
Christopher J. Pole, and Robert G. Burgess

INTRODUCTION

Computers have, for a long time, formed part of the qualitative researcher's range of research tools, but mainly for word processing purposes. In the last decade a number of "chunking and coding"[1] computer software packages have come on to the market, all with the objective of assisting the qualitative researcher with data analysis. It is often stressed that these packages have been developed demand-led, by qualitative researchers searching for ways to improve the quality of their research and not by the big computer software houses in search of profitable trade. So what needs does the qualitative research community have which

Studies in Qualitative Methodology, Volume 5, pages 81-104.

ISBN: 1-55938-902-8.

it is hoped can be met by the introduction of the use of computer software? Authors have summed up potential benefits in existing literature on using qualitative software in research. For example, "we can think about the computer in helping in these two ways: in enhancing what we already do, and in opening up new possibilities" (Dey 1993, p. 55). Alternatively, "it is likely that computers will bring real benefits to qualitative researchers, making their work easier, more productive and potentially more thorough" (Fielding and Lee 1992, p. 6). Qualitative researchers are not completely satisfied with the processes and mechanics they currently use to analyze data. There is a need for more efficiency, less repetition, more reliability in recording, storing, filing, indexing, and retrieving—in short, managing data. The computer can deliver this, but more importantly, it can also add new dimensions to research. These new dimensions include the ability to interrogate data and revise conceptualizations through the endless cross-data searches which can be carried out and the possibilities for linking all types of data, indices, and glossaries. Richards and Richards have called this the introduction of "more subtle, varied, powerful and rigorous ways of doing what the method[2] has always attempted to do" (1992, p. 53). In addition, computer software can make it easier to account for analytic processes which have taken place and to show the procedures on which results are based. In this sense, some believe, computer-based analysis might set new standards in the reporting of qualitative research (Dey 1993, p. 60).

Of the many packages currently available ACQUAD, The Ethnograph, and NUD•IST, are the most extensively used (for a basic description of the software available see Fielding and Lee 1992, pp. 195-199). Possibilities for receiving (technical) training in the use of the software have increased as well as the number of publications primarily discussing the "nuts and bolts" of using the respective software in research (Richards and Richards 1994; Tesch 1990). It has taken some time, however, before detailed accounts of the use of these packages in practice, and in the context of specific projects, have started to appear (Macguire 1990). Few publications on qualitative research software focus on analysis of research data, and when they do they tend to do so from a general perspective (Lee and Fielding 1992; Dey 1993). The lack of detailed descriptions of how the computer has played a role in data analysis does not come as a surprise as qualitative researchers have a history of putting data collection procedures at center stage, reducing the analysis of data collected to a relatively minor role. As Bryman and Burgess have observed:

> ... just as qualitative researchers have in the last two decades developed methods of data collection, so the challenge for qualitative researchers in the next decade is to articulate as fully as possible the processes associated with data analysis (Bryman and Burgess 1994, p. 224).

It is generally acknowledged that for all too long the emphasis in publications on qualitative research has been on the organization of fieldwork: gaining access, data collection strategies, and fieldwork relationships. Approaches to data analysis received relatively little attention. However, Bryman and Burgess point out that the failure to address data analysis as an important issue in itself is no longer universal given recent work of, among others, Miles and Huberman (1994), Strausss (1987), Tesch (1990), and Fielding and Lee (1992). The aim of this paper is to contribute to the literature on data analysis in qualitative research by examining how the use of qualitative software conditioned the analysis in our study of postgraduate students in the natural sciences and engineering.

THE PROJECT

This paper is based on the use of The Ethnograph[3] software package in the analysis of data collected in our project that examined the process of becoming a first-year Ph.D. student in physics, mathematics, and engineering. Nine departments in higher education institutions, three in each discipline, were selected according to the following criteria: research selectivity rating in 1992, number of doctoral students, subject areas covered, and geographical location. Data were collected in the form of documentary evidence; interviews with Ph.D. students, supervisors, deans of school, registrars, and other key personnel;

as well as field notes and observational data produced during visits to departments. The interviews with students and supervisors formed the bulk of the data. These key players were interviewed for between three quarters of an hour to an hour. In the interviews with students the following issues were covered: the student's background, the student's view of the Ph.D. experience in the first year, and commitment to the institution/discipline/research group. In view of the sheer volume and complexity of the data gathered (112 interviews) this seemed an excellent opportunity to explore the use of a qualitative computer software package for data analysis and The Ethnograph feature which allowed for extensive multiple code searches gave the package the edge in the project team's decision on which software to use.

THE PROGRAM

John Seidel has described how the need for The Ethnograph arose for him and a fellow graduate student:

> We barely survived transcribing on typewriters, and then manually cutting and pasting multiple Xeroxed copies of our data. During this experience we came to the conclusion that there had to be a better way (Seidel et al. 1988, p. i).

The Ethnograph manual claims that it will provide a better way of analyzing data in that it will perform "some of the mechanical tasks in a way that free the researcher from these chores and allowing him or her to think about and analyse data in a more creative and intricate way" (Seidel et al. 1988).

Basically, the program works in the following way. A collection of data, for example, an interview, is typed into a word processing document. This is then formatted (converted) into The Ethnograph form, as a result of which the right-hand part of a page is left empty for future notes by the researcher. The researcher then instructs the program to number each line of text and print the document out. The researcher subsequently codes (this is an Ethnograph term, basically describing a process of making notes in the form of categories or labels) the printout.[4] Codes can be amended or modified any time. The document is shown on the screen or printed as two areas:

their talk (material)	the researcher's talk about their talk.

When searches are carried out using any one of the codes, both areas are displayed. The following example shows a section of a transcribed interview with a particle physics Ph.D. student (the material) and the researcher's talk about their talk in the form of codes.

Example 1

```
TAPENUMBER: 24     DISCIPLINE:  PHYSICS   SUBFIELD:  PARTICLE
AGE:       -23     GENDER:      M         PHD        YEAR: 1

E: $-APPLYING

SC: +CHOICE -INSTITUTIO

£-POLITICS £-TACTICS £-CHOICE %-PARTICLE %-PHYSICS *-SELFREFLEC
*-INTEREST
: AM And did you only apply for a PhD in   250 -£ |  -%  -*
:    particle physics or ?                 251  £ |   |   |
:                                               £ |   |   |
:                                               £ |   |   |
:   S1 Yes I did, yes. Again I mean it's   254  £ |   |   |
:    probably a slightly lazy attitude I   255  £ |   |   |
:    just felt that it was as good as      256  £ |   |   |
:    anything as far as I was concerned.   257  £ |   |  -*
:    No this is something I've always felt 258  £ |   |
:    that if you put down three or four    259  £ |   |
:    different Ph.Ds on your application   260  £ |   |
:    sometimes - I don't know if this is   261  £ |   |
:    true - you feel that maybe you'll be  262  £ |   |
:    given a second or third place on the  263  £ |   |
:    listing because you haven't defined   264  £ |   |
:    what your choice will be. So I        265  £ |   |
:    suppose that balances into it,        266  £ |   |
:    tactical decision.                    267 -£ |   |
```

The idea is, by "handing the data over to the computer," the cutting associated with non computer-based data analysis will be abolished and searching and sorting will become more systematic. Although it is acknowledged that the researcher has to be involved in the manipulation of the data in order to stay in touch with it, those advocating the use of the program do not generally suggest that any dimension to the research process might be lost by allocating "mechanical" tasks to the computer (an exception is Seidel 1992). The changes that might occur are presented in a positive light. For example, time saved because the computer performs mechanical tasks can be spent more effectively on the critical interpretative aspects of data analysis. It has to be borne in mind, however, that saving time is definitely not the only issue to be considered. The real issue concerning qualitative software is whether it enhances the process of analysis. In this paper we are particularly concerned with whether the use of The Ethnograph changes the nature, sequence, or process of data analysis.

METHOD

In our case using The Ethnograph for the first time on a research project came in a series of steps. They were:

1. Reading the manual and getting to know the program;
2. Making a decision on the data to be loaded on, bringing the files containing the data into the right format;
3. Coding the transcripts by hand;
4. Coding the transcriptions into the computer, and setting up templates needed to create face sheets. Face sheets attach an identifier to each file, opening up possibilities for searches according to variables such as gender or year of study as well as defining the file containing the interview or event which has come up in a search.
5. Searching, sorting, and building on coded segments.

1. Reading the Manual and Getting to Know the Program

This phase can be very time consuming particularly if there is nobody around with experience using the program. For someone with few computer skills (for example only basic word processing experience as would be the case with most qualitative researchers), the absence of a computer support person could easily make the hurdle of this first stage insurmountable. Apart from the technical difficulties which might be encountered in loading the program onto a suitable computer and learning simple tasks like making copies of formatted, numbered, and coded files, some knowledge of the technical side of the package is important to be able to make informed decisions about what use to make of the software. In our experience it is essential to make sure that the basics behind the program are understood before making decisions as to how to use it. The manual is not well written but quite user-friendly. However, it takes time to digest all the information and as in all projects, time is at a premium. Due to other pressing commitments of researchers, secretarial staff, and the computing officer we had to turn to for advice there were long periods in which the program could hardly be used because the relevant person in the chain was unavailable and the work could not be continued without that person's help. In terms of our limited experience we were very reliant on each other's newly acquired skills and as a result of that it took us seven months to get up and running.

2. Making a Decision on the Data to Be Loaded On, Bringing the Data into the Right Format

Our research involved different sets of data: documents, interviews with students, supervisors and others involved in postgraduate education as well as field notes. It would have been possible to "read" all documents with a laser, code them and feed them into the computer in The Ethnograph format. As we had lost so much time in setting up the program and learning how to work with it we decided to limit the use of The Ethnograph to interviews. The last decision was made midway through the project with the objective of reviewing this decision a few months later during an interim evaluation of setting the time The Ethnograph had cost against the benefits it would bring. We thought the number of student transcripts were sufficient to allow for a proper evaluation of the package. In practice, because of the time it took to process the transcripts and set up and get to know The Ethnograph we reached the evaluation stage for the student transcripts only in the last few months of the project. Although the project involved field notes from team members they were never processed through The Ethnograph software package. In the end more than one-half of all the interviews conducted, that is, mainly student interview transcripts, were loaded and coded into The Ethnograph. This means that data sets within The Ethnograph were never complete and always had to be examined in conjunction with other data elsewhere.

Interviews which were to be used with The Ethnograph first needed to be transcribed. In a project like ours, in which tapes are transcribed and the costs associated with this work have already been calculated into the project budget, this does not in itself involve a lot of extra work. It did not take the project secretary long to work out how to translate Microsoft Word documents into The Ethnograph format and print them out. Without secretarial support, however, this process would make enormous time demands on a researcher as all interviews would have to be transcribed fully by the researcher or typed in the form of a verbal account/field notes. Even in our case, the speed by which the part-time project secretary could produce the tapes could not keep up with the number of tapes coming in as a result of three people going regularly on field trips. This caused a serious time lag between an interview being conducted and the transcript becoming available and, therefore, also slowed down the speed with which transcripts could be hand and then computer-coded. This was only acknowledged by the project team at a late stage in the project and a temporary secretary was brought in to transcribe the backlog of tapes. Of course, this problem would also have occurred in a project which did not use qualitative software. However, if our point is accepted that the nature and sequence of the analytic process when using qualitative software differs from non-computer based processes of analysis then the late processing of transcripts may be more significant than becomes clear at first glance.

3-4. Coding the Transcripts by Hand and Subsequently Feeding the Codes into the Computer, After Adding on the Templates

The main aim of The Ethnograph is to assist with the analysis of data, through sorting coded data, although the process of coding itself remains the exclusive activity of the researcher. Coding is a very important activity within the research process as it serves to provide the structure within which data are first organized. More importantly, coding also represents the first step in the conceptualization of data.

The set up of The Ethnograph means that once the transcripts have been reformatted into a numbered version, the document has to be printed out and the researcher codes the transcripts by hand with fine detail to the start and finish lines of the code(s). This process involves going through the transcripts by hand, and the coding schemes on paper subsequently need to be transferred to the computer. The Ethnograph does not allow coding straight into the computer because you cannot see the text you are actually coding when you feed the codes in. All you have in front of you on the screen is a box in which you type your start line, code word, and finish line. Technically it should be possible to create the possibility of immediate computer coding and this would certainly reduce the workload. In our case, copying coding schemes on paper onto the computer was done by the researchers themselves. Funding permitting this could be done by clerical staff.

Apart from the extra work involved in paper and computer coding, the precision required and the restrictions the form of the codes are under makes the researcher spend more time on the initial coding process than he or she would when using non-computer based methods. Coding the transcripts on paper for The Ethnograph means analytic categories have to be restricted to 10 letter words or combinations of words which means that the codes have to be considered carefully before being included and abbreviations thought through. The 10-letter word restriction is probably a technical requirement as the code needs to fit the space left for the researcher's reflections on the program. In our project there were two basic difficulties with the coding, one was the necessity to continuously discuss coding schemes, the other was how to overcome simple typing errors or other technical mistakes, which complicate the use of The Ethnograph.

If different people work with the same transcripts without The Ethnograph there is no need to keep on top of each other's conceptualizations and developments of thoughts continuously and consistently. Without any pre-existing knowledge, researchers can read each other's notes and examine cuttings visually. However, when using The Ethnograph several people share the use of the researchers' space to make notes and conduct searches on the basis of those notes. As re-coded notes cannot be located by searching for the original code it is important to have some idea of what other researchers had been adding to and modifying in the data (researcher's notes) to maximize retrievability of data.

In our experience coding needs to be kept recorded to make sure there is coherence throughout the transcripts. The effect of being able to retrieve information more systematically is lost if different codes are used for the same phenomena. Simple mistakes like using plurals for some words and singular terms for others mean that the program will only pick out the one set of codes when searching. The ease with which such coding mistakes are made can be brought back to the tendency to use the same words and terms as the interviewee has used. For example, using "observe," "observing," and "observation," or "topic" and "project," "dedication" and "commitment" for the same subject matter.

One way in which the team overcame these problems was to record every code used in a "code book" so that when it came to searching we had a clear record of all the codes we had used. This, however, is also extremely time consuming and does lead to an increase in the kind of mechanical tasks The Ethnograph aims to eliminate. Despite the quickness and ease with which a correction can be made and the availability of a printout of the code sets for each transcript this is a serious time wasting feature of using The Ethnograph 3.0. The new version, that is reported to have a dictionary of codes which can be brought up on the screen, might be a great improvement in this respect. In addition, a thesaurus type facility should be technically possible and would be very helpful.

In order to comply with these stringent coding requirements, there is a tendency on the part of the researcher not to interpret what is actually being said by developing ideas and concepts while reading transcripts, but to concentrate on looking for that "buzz" word which will trigger a familiar code. This attitude is the result of the psychological process accompanying the notion of leaving the mechanical tasks to the computer. In this phase of computer coding the researcher becomes obsessed with feeding the right information into the computer so that data do not "get lost." In that sense the reading of transcripts becomes a technical rather than a "thinking" exercise. In our experience coding with The Ethnograph therefore had the effect of delaying innovative and critical thinking until after all transcripts had been coded the first time around.

Any research based on relatively small sets of data may mean that a researcher's memory is probably strong enough to recall details of interviews and to allow association processes to take place across the data. The use of The Ethnograph in this type of project would probably generate a lot of extra work without bringing benefits. Any research that involves a large number of transcripts (interviews or field notes) would have to bc viewed in relation to the amount of time the researcher has to spare to work with The Ethnograph as obviously the more transcripts there would be to code the more time would have to be spent in the computer coding process. The crucial question therefore is: how much time does The Ethnograph subsequently save in the searching and selecting element of the research? And even more importantly, can it deepen and enrich the process of data analysis so that the extra time spent on computer coding and organization of data can be justified?

5. Searching and Sorting Coded Segments

As Bryman and Burgess have pointed out, there is the potential for considerable confusion regarding what coding exactly is (Bryman and Burgess 1994, p. 218). The perceptions that researchers have of coding has an impact on the analytical goals set for that process. The opposite ends of the spectrum of outcomes (or the two extremes of this process) are "data retrieval" and "theory discovery."

In the case of "data retrieval," coding is the process through which segments of data records are identified in a systematic way so that this data can be retrieved at a later stage. Rather than being instrumental in developing theory, this type of coding is aimed primarily at theory testing:

> All codes are systematically applied to label segments for retrieval. That all text is thus coded is essential for the theory testing goal; ultimately, any emerging pattern can and must be tested by retrieving *all* the instances that fit the theory (Richards and Richards 1992, p. 44).

"Theory discovery" on the other hand, results from "open coding" for theory generation. Qualitative researchers aiming to generate theory through coding processes work on the basis of the method of "grounded theory" that is the "discovery of theory from data" as developed by Glaser and Strauss (1967). Open coding is a process in which data and concepts are fitted together, and those concepts amended constantly. As Bryman and Burgess point out, although many qualitative researchers have reported on conceptualization in their analyses, the extent to which theory is being generated is open to discussion (Bryman and Burgess 1994). In that respect "concept discovery" (Martin and Turner 1986) is probably a more appropriate term for describing the goals researchers have set for themselves while coding their data. As Miles and Huberman have argued (1994) even the identification of descriptive codes is part of a theorizing process. The codes inserted with the objective of retrieval organize the data in a certain way and in that sense determine what is later going to be retrieved and what is not. Do we identify the supervisor of the student concerned on the template (the label to be attached to each section of a transcript which is printed or comes up on screen) so that we can analyze their statements in relation to each other? Do we include codes on the physical environment? Is the latter relevant for the process of becoming a Ph.D. student and so on. To illustrate the importance of, for example, the choice of variables in the following template[5] follows a short coded version of text with two different templates and the variables they consist of.

Example 2

TEMPLATE 1
TAPE 3

```
DISCIPLINE:  ENGINEERING              SUBFIELD:  OCEANOGRAPH
AGE:     23      GENDER:      MALE          SUPERVISOR:  TAPE78
NATIONALITY:  BRITISH
```

TEMPLATE 2
TAPE 3

```
DISCIPLINE:  ENGINEERING               SUBFIELD:  OCEANOGRAPH
UNIVERSITY:  NO.8     UG AT UNI:  YES              YEAR OF STUDY:  3
EXPERIMENTAL WORK:  NO
```

(UG AT UNI = undergraduate at the same university)

```
SC:  +ROLESUPERV      +EXPECTATIO

£-ROLESUPERV              £-EXPECTATIO

     :  Right. I mean what would you expect      1427    -£
     :  his role to be within your Ph.D?         1428     £
     :                                                    £
     :                                                    £
     :  I'd expect him to be very much the       1431     £
     :  same as what it has been up to date.     1432     £
     :  But maybe to be a bit - see like he's    1433     £
$-PRESSURE          $-CLOSTAB $-CONTROL
     :  perhaps not as forceful as I would       1434     £   -$
     :  like in the way that he doesn't sort     1435     £    |
     :  of say 'you know you really should get   1436     £    |
     :  cracking' or 'you really should of try   1437     £    |
%-SUPERVISOR       %-DIRECTION
     :  to work on sections.' You know he        1438     £    |    -%
     :  sort of like I put forward a few ideas   1439     £    |     |
     :  and he says 'well yes,' he sort of       1440     £    |     |
     :  moulds it a bit but he doesn't mould   1441  £    |    |
     :  it as agressively as I probably like.    1442     £    |     |
```

Whatever objectives one has in mind with respect to coding, The Ethnograph is meant to support the whole range of applications of coding. Searching for data (retrieval of information) and facilitating the development of analytical concepts through a relatively straightforward process of coding and recoding, adding and deleting, comparison and modification are the processes for which the package was designed and, therefore, where the researcher should find the most gains of working with the program.

The code retrieval or searching facility has a number of options so the researcher can get the maximum data needed. In principle, using either the single or multiple searches the researcher can get hold of relevant data without having to sift through every transcript by hand. This obviously is an enormous advantage over non-computer methods of analysis where this sifting is unavoidable. There was only one problem that became immediately apparent in our first attempts to compare sets of data through searches. The data that has been selected by the computer via the codes which the researcher asks it to search for can often seem out of context. This was especially noticeable if following the manual guidelines of "netting" the codes, that is, placing codes inside of other codes so that some codes only cover a couple of lines, which limits the data that is retrieved, rather than grouping codes together so that they cover a whole passage or an entire answer to a question. Retrieving the data in the context that it was said or written is essential for better understanding and to take it away from this setting could lead to a misinterpretation of data.

Example 3

"FAMILY" CODE IS NETTED

TAPE48 IB Because

DISCIPLINE: PHYSICS SUBFIELD: PARTICLE AGE: 23
PHD YEAR: 1 UG AT UNIV: Y PT/FT: FT

E: *-LECTURING
E: %-INDUSTRY %-MOTIVATION
E: £-FUTURE £-CAREER £-ACADEMIA

SC: FAMILY

(continued)

Example 3. (Continued)

```
$-FAMILY      $-FATHER      $-BACKGROUND
     : just don't want to do that. Also I      1073  | -$ |   |
     : just want to move on. I come from a     1074  |  $ |   |
     : very working class family and - well I  1075  |  $ |   |
     : disagree with my father every time he   1076  |  $ |   |
     : tells me to go and get a 'real' job I   1077  |  $ |   |
     : guess somewhere in my subconscious      1078  |  $ |   |
     : there's always something telling me     1079  |  $ |   |
     : that I haven't got a real job until      1080  |  $ |   |
     : I've worked in industry. The money's    1081  | -$ |   |
```

'FAMILY' CODE IS NOT NETTED

```
TAPE48        IB Because
--------------------------------------------------------------------
DISCIPLINE:  PHYSICS       SUBFIELD:  PARTICLE      AGE: 23
PHD YEAR:  1               UG AT UNIV:  Y           PT/FT: FT

E:  *-LECTURING
E:  %-INDUSTRY         %-MOTIVATION
E:  £-FUTURE           £-CAREER       £-ACADEMIA

SC: FAMILY

%-FAMILY  %-BACKGROUND  %-INDUSTRY  %-MOTIVATION
     : give lectures in front of people. I      1070  |       -% |
     : could do it I'm sure, people have told   1071  |        % |
     : me I could do it quite well too but I    1072  |        % |
$-FAMILY  $-FATHER  $-BACKGROUND
     : just don't want to do that. Also I       1073  | -$     % |
     : just want to move on. I come from a      1074  |  |     % |
     : very working class family and - well I   1075  |  |     % |
     : disagree with my father every time he    1076  |  |     % |
     : tells me to go and get a 'real' job I    1077  |  |     % |
     : guess somewhere in my subconscious       1078  |  |     % |
     : there's always something telling me      1079  |  |     % |
     : that I haven't got a real job until       1080  | -$     % |
     : I've worked in industry. The money's     1081  |        % |
     : better of course and I can't see         1082  |        % |
     : myself wanting to do research and        1083  |        % |
     : development for my whole life, I'm       1084  |        % |
     : glad that I've done it you know that     1085  |        % |
     : I've done it so I want to move on, I     1086  |        % |
     : want to move up the ladder as it were.   1087  |        % |
```

Through a face sheet and/or code search, The Ethnograph can normally quickly pinpoint the section of the data that the researcher is interested in, at least as long as the coding has been carried out consistently, so if needed it is possible to go back to the paper versions of the transcripts. We found we did that anyway to avoid having to make excessive printouts of all searches. The alternative, working with the text on the screen and moving from one transcript to the next was tiring, giving us a sense of not being in control. It also reduced the number of team members who could work with the data at any given time to one. The feeling that we were not in control was strengthened by certain features of The Ethnograph, among them, the fact that it is difficult to skip data in searches, or to go back to the previous screen so one spends a lot of time pressing buttons and staring at a flickering screen. In addition, there is continuously a decision to be made about whether or not to print results of a search. Let us say a search on the basis of a certain combination of keywords leads the researcher to consider a reconceptualization, for example, whether or not to develop the notion of "real work" in the analysis of supervisors' attitudes toward postgraduate research. Without printing out the segments of text just found or making detailed notes of the search carried out, it might be difficult to do some more searches and then subsequently get back confirmed in the idea of developing this notion of "real work." Unless we recoded first we found it troublesome to find the same segment again without including notes on the search pattern followed. Here one has to balance the need to avoid making endless printouts against the time it costs to make extensive notes so as not to forget aspects of the search. Maybe more experienced users of The Ethnograph have found a way around this, but it is significant that, in 20 months, we did not manage to overcome this dilemma in a satisfactory way. We still ended up with a complex set of notes and comments, reminders, code books, printouts, and so on that we kept outside The Ethnograph package because we had the feeling of not being in control if we were dependent on the notes and the data on disk. Although the full use of the package had required our complete commitment and a lot of our time that safe feeling of being on top of the computerized data, of being fully acquainted with it, and being able to play with it, never really came through. The set of paper notes and materials formed the basis for an essential part of our analysis. In the end we always went back to a paper transcript, not only at the writing stage but also several times during analysis.

During the writing stage we encountered problems with the fact that the researcher needs to use the PC where The Ethnograph is loaded as a word processor to write with. It is therefore impossible to keep the selections of a transcript on screen while writing. Printing out all relevant sections of a transcript we found to be both excessive and wasteful of paper. Of course The Ethnograph clearly shows where each section of data can be found, but it is a cumbersome process to make a note of where the section of data can be found in the papered version of the transcript and so to work from that in the process of writing. This is another example of the process through which The Ethnograph leads to an increase in mechanical tasks. If one regularly has to go back to the paper transcript in detail after all, what is the point of using the program? A researcher who has coded transcripts manually will very often be in a position to remember certain aspects of the data and go back to them in the transcripts without the help of The Ethnograph.

DID WE BENEFIT FROM USING THE ETHNOGRAPH IN TERMS OF TIME OR QUALITY OF ANALYSIS?

The central questions are: is the process of analysis through The Ethnograph less time consuming in principle, and, of better quality under certain conditions?

Time

On the basis of the above discussion of our research with The Ethnograph, our preliminary conclusion on the first part of the question is negative in our case. Although the software did some chores for us, thus freeing our time to do other things, it introduced others. The time needed to become Ethnograph literate was considerable and we certainly have not managed to master the package completely although two research team members and a secretary devoted a considerable amount of time to it. Apart from reading the manual, getting to know the program, setting up the package, sorting out problems, organizing back-up copies, discussing the data in meetings, and more importantly, starting the process of recoding and searching, the researchers spent an average of five hours and 20 minutes on hand-coding an interview of an hour and then feeding these initial coding schemes into the computer. Similarly, after having become familiar with the program, the project secretary spent 10 hours and 35 minutes on processing an interview of one hour: transcribing, re-formatting, printing out, and copying between machines and onto floppy discs. However, we would hope that these times could be improved upon with increased familiarity with the program.

Quality of Analysis

Of course quality of analysis in any one project is dependent on the quality of the data and the skills of the researcher. The use of The Ethnograph can only maximize those qualities but not exceed them. This is an obvious and indeed important restriction of the program which should form the basis of any attempt to answer the second question. Whether, compensating for the negative answer to the first question in the case of our research project, The Ethnograph coding, sorting, and searching processes are more effective in concept and theory building than non-computer based methods of analysis. However, the way in which the team benefited from using the package overall is very difficult to explore without tracing the way papers developed in detail. Some remarks, however, can be made.

We found that in our project the The Ethnograph slowed down the interpretative part of analysis and had the effect of separating it more rigorously from the mechanical parts of analysis. Reflecting on it now, a "code-first, think-next" pattern developed, similar to processes in survey research (Richards and Richards 1992, p. 50). As a result of this movement between the data, concept definition and other phases in the process of analysis were only entered into when the transcript was fully coded in the machine. Then, in computer form, a transcript was no longer easily accessible as a whole, and basically tended to be used in parts. This meant that thinking about an interview as a whole was often replaced by thinking across the data.

A COMPLICATING FACTOR: TEAM RESEARCH

The fact that The Ethnograph was used in team research is a very important factor to be considered in evaluating its use. We found that The Ethnograph has some facets which complicate team research. First, all members of a team need to work very closely together in coding the transcripts. For most team research it would probably be impractical for the whole team to sit together coding, at least for the start of the coding process, but a high degree of coordination is necessary if all members of the team are going to be able to use the package. Our choice was to load all data onto one machine which was available to all members of the team. The alternative, with every member of the team having their own machine and doing their own coding and subsequent cutting, pasting, sorting, commenting, and deleting would have introduced too much extra work. Moreover, it was decided that using two machines but copying each piece of work onto the other so that two people could work simultaneously while building onto each other's work would take too much in terms of project organization. We could think of no watertight scheme to make it impossible to make mistakes and confuse versions. This was in addition to the fact that the machines that were able to hold the package were already in great demand in the center and competition to work on them tough. One machine, coordination of working hours, a rigid division of labor, and coordinated,—sometimes joint—coding was the result. This had the benefit that only one backup copy of data needed to be made and there was not the confusion over which machine contained the most recent coded transcript for analysis. On the other hand, this meant that codes had to be worked out using rigid guidelines, because otherwise incoherencies would occur making searches incomplete and cross transcript comparisons impossible. To set up basic coding schemes which were to be used as a first step, three team members coded a few transcripts and passed them on to each other. Once these codes were in place, one researcher stopped being involved in The Ethnograph coding and the rest of the coding was carried out by the two remaining researchers who kept a note on the time spent on activities such as hand coding, computer coding, and searches. The division of work in the team was such that individual members of the team took it upon themselves to write a first draft of a paper on issues which arose during team meetings and discussions. As a result of the division of work on The Ethnograph a pattern developed which mentally separated the team members working with the package and those who did not.

The team members intensively involved in processing data through The Ethnograph wrote a first version of a paper which, for several reasons, some of them unrelated to The Ethnograph, was very quantitative in nature in the early drafts. The software was used to develop categories of fields of influence which played a role in their decision to start a Ph.D. These categories were: "love of subject," "stay on," "ultimate intellectual challenge," "career move," and "second choice." Individual students were subsequently placed into these categories on the basis of code word searches of transcripts, and conclusions drawn from the results. The other team members felt uneasy with this approach as they considered that their colleagues having spent so much of their time on The Ethnograph, had been tempted to do qualitative research in a quantitative way. A "counting numbers" type of approach had been a logical next step in view of the fact that sorting and cutting processes had been mechanized. The original paper was subsequently transformed (Sprokkereef, Lakin, Pole, and Burgess 1994) and counting students completely abolished.

Our feeling was that, in contrast to Seidel's statement that The Ethnograph 3.0 would allow us "to devote more time and attention" to the critical aspects of qualitative data analysis, freeing us from mechanical aspects of the work, it did not free us at all. It simply substituted one set of tools with another.

Moreover, the fact that the team member not extensively involved in The Ethnograph wrote a paper on supervision on the basis of all documentation, field notes, and the uncoded interviews on paper would suggest that the use of the computer in analysis is not only a matter of technical skills, but also of "culture." Habits of years cannot easily be changed, but in addition, the use of computers in research is traditionally looked at with suspicion within qualitative research circles. Although qualitative software developers might argue there is a need for computer-aided facilities, individual researchers in practice might not feel like that. The team subsequently decided that The Ethnograph was to be used to provide examples. In this respect, the software did not help interpret data or develop concepts but just served to illustrate processes already described and identified. Some would argue this is exactly what The Ethnograph is for, nothing more and nothing less. It is certainly not the only use it is meant for according to the software developers. Using The Ethnograph in this way alone reduces the package to a retrieval mechanism, without its "enabler" features in the interpretative work of cutting and pasting, in the interpretation of processes and the categorization or comparison of segments of text and so on (Seidel 1988, pp. 1-4).

In view of the amount of work which actually goes into loading coded transcripts into The Ethnograph it is definitely a waste of resources if all data have been processed in that way and not all members of a team use it for data analysis and writing.

To use The Ethnograph in team research is most beneficial if the whole team can use the package to its full potential with competence, and for this to happen each team member would have to be able to spend at least a few weeks on the machine. This would mean introducing new divisions of work and a change of practice in data analysis in a team context. It would also involve sponsors paying for more secretarial support or additional researcher's time to analyze the data. Although in this project the secretary was very capable, interested in computers and their applications, and dedicated to the project, her time was limited, yet personally made enormous contributions to the project. For a team to be able to use The Ethnograph effectively, a dedicated full-time secretary, working closely with the team is essential.

It is remarkable that in all the literature, the shortcomings of packages such as The Ethnograph receive relatively little attention.

This might well be because those writing about it have developed these programs or are involved in giving courses instructing others on how to use them, but have rarely actually used a package in a "real" project of one or two years duration. Many improvements of these packages must be possible which would remove many of the problems we have encountered. For example, it should be technically possible to code straight into the PC, reading a transcript on screen and superimposing the codes. This would both save time and increase the researcher's sense of being in charge of the data. Also, a coding dictionary or thesaurus to call up previously used codes on screen should be relatively easy to develop as an extra facility. This would save the researcher from having to make extensive use of notes or even setting up a "code book." It must also be possible to create a search procedure which allows you to hop back a few segments with a touch of a button, without having to start a search all over again. However, we have not even discussed advances in technology such as machines which are able to transcribe interviews like a tape recorder and register conversations. We are waiting in anticipation.

ACKNOWLEDGMENTS

The authors would like to acknowledge the assistance of the project secretary Mrs. Sylvia Moore in helping the development of their understanding of the ETHNOGRAPH.

NOTES

1. This paper is written on the basis of the use of a "chunking and coding" program, a term taken from Tesch (1992, pp. 16-37). She discusses the range of available software for qualitative data analysis including text management databases, concordance programs, and "qualitative modeling" programs. The basic character of a "chunking and coding" program is that text to be analyzed is typed into the computer, segments of interest to the analyst are coded, and the segments can be retrieved and recoded.
2. Qualitative method.
3. The Ethnograph, version 3.0, developed by John Seidel, is available from Qualis Research Associates, Corvallis. One copy of the program costs

approximately $150. The program allows the researcher to identify and retrieve text from documents. A maximum of 12 "code words" are allowed per unit of text. Bits of text can be nested and overlapped seven levels deep and searches can be made across the seven levels. Modifications of the code words, that is, recoding possible and data files can be searched in sets on the basis of labels (templates) designed by the researcher (Seidel et al. 1988).

4. The activity of coding means different things to different people (see for example Bryman and Burgess 1994, p. 5; Richards and Richards 1992, p. 44). Seidel himself has expressed regret at using the word coding in The Ethnograph manual (1992, p. 112).

5. Although variables of templates can be amended later, it is a cumbersome procedure in which researchers have to reconstruct all templates of previously processed transcripts.

REFERENCES

Bryman, A., and R. Burgess (Eds).
1994 *Analysing Qualitative Data*. London: Routledge.

Burgess, R.
1984 *In the Field: An Introduction to Field Research*. London: Allen and Unwin.

Dey, I.
1993 *Qualitative Data Analysis*. London: Routledge.

Fielding, N., and R.M. Lee (Eds).
1992 *Using Computers in Qualitative Research*. London: Sage.

Glaser, B., and A. Strauss
1967 *The Discovery of Grounded Theory*. Chicago: Aldine.

Macguire, J., and D. Botting
1990 "The Use of the Ethnograph Program to Identify Perceptions of Nursing Staff Following the Introduction of Primary Nursing in an Acute Medical Ward for Elderly People." *Journal of Advanced Nursing* 15(10): 1120-1127.

Martin, P., and B. Turner
1986 "Grounded Theory and Organisational Research." *Journal of Applied Behaviour* 22(2): 141-157.

Miles, M., and M. Huberman
1994 *Qualitative Data Analysis*, 2nd ed. Beverley Hills: Sage.

Pfaffenberger, B.
1988 *Microcomputer Applications in Qualitative Research*. London: Sage.

Pole, C., A. Sprokkereef, R. Burgess, and E. Lakin
1994 "Supervision of Doctoral Students in the Natural Sciences: Expectations and Experiences." Paper presented at the UK Council for

Graduate Education 2nd Summer Conference, University of Nottingham.

Richards, L., and T. Richards
1992 "The Transformation of Qualitative Method: Computational Paradigms and Research Processes." Pp.38-53 in *Using Computers in Qualitative Research*, edited by N. Fielding and R.M. Lee. London: Sage.

Richards, L., and T. Richards
1994 "From Filing Cabinet to Computer." Pp.146-172 in *Analysing Qualitative Data*, edited by A. Bryman and R. Burgess. London: Routledge.

Seidel, J.
1992 "Methods and Madness in the Application of Computer Technology to Qualitative Data Analysis." Pp.107-116 in *Using Computers in Qualitative Research*, edited by N. Fielding and R.M. Lee. London: Sage.

Seidel, J., R. Kjolseth, and E. Seymour
1988 *The Ethnograph a User's Guide*. Corvallis: Qualis Research Associates.

Sprokkereef, A., E. Lakin, C. Pole, and R. Burgess
1994 "Why Physics Students Start Doctorates: Fouteen Years On." CEDAR unpublished paper.

Strauss, A.
1987 *Qualitative Analysis for Social Scientists*. Cambridge: Cambridge University Press.

Tesch, R.
1990 *Qualitative Research: Analysis Types and Software Tools*. London: Falmer Press.

Tesch, R.
1992 "Software for Qualitative Researchers: Analysis Needs and Program Capabilities." Pp.16-37 in *Using Computers in Qualitative Research*, edited by N. Fielding and R.M. Lee. London: Sage.

TRANSITION WORK! REFLECTIONS ON A THREE-YEAR NUD•IST PROJECT

Lyn Richards

INTRODUCTION

The debate about *whether* to compute in qualitative research seems to be over. It never really began. The advantages of computers for managing messy data records are obvious, wherever variety of records and richness of accounts challenge researchers. All researchers working in the qualitative mode will be clearly helped by some computer software. To avoid using computers now disadvantages particularly those whose data records are rich, or whose research attempts to contribute confident results, not merely reports in terms of "signposts for future research." But because the advantages of computers are now so pertinent to the methods

Studies in Qualitative Methodology, Volume 5, pages 105-140.

ISBN: 1-55938-902-8.

of qualitative researchers, and computing so unavoidable for most researchers, it is essential that the literature address the new challenges researchers meet with qualitative computing (Richards and Richards 1991a, 1991b).

Qualitative research, with or without computers, is often reported with little attention to the processes of management of data and theory construction. Qualitative computing promised to change this, stimulating a debate about handling data. There has indeed been considerable discussion about what computers contribute. An early pioneer in this methodological discussion was Renata Tesch (1990), whose contributions and energetic enthusiasm will now be sadly missed. She stressed the use of computers for *organizing systems*. More recently, discussions have addressed a wider range of ways by which creativity, as well as organization, can be supported by computers (Fielding and Lee, this volume; Richards and Richards 1994b; Weitzman and Miles 1995). But there is still little critical assessment of what the computer *did* in real projects. Reports often merely name the software used as though this explains and justifies the method, and give little idea as to how it assisted or hindered research (*Qualitative Sociology* 1991). Since qualitative research is now so inevitably moving to computing, the continuation of critical debate is crucial, and it must include consideration of effects on the research and the researchers.

This paper reports on one such project and the possibilities and challenges the computer software permitted and presented. The project provides a fine laboratory for such reflection, as it set out to exploit software designed not just for organizing data, but also for exploring the relation between data and ideas, and removing constraints to both. Its design also strained the normal bounds of qualitative research, requiring a variety of data sources, longitudinal development, and large numbers of responses. Computer software does not of course require that projects are so designed, but it permits them to be. So projects pursuing these possibilities dramatically display the new challenges of qualitative computing. The team learned from, and reflected on, these challenges over three years.

The present report draws on that experience, quoting from papers written at the time, in particular from a detailed account prepared in the final year of the project (Richards and Simon 1993) and a conference paper delivered in the following year by five members of the team (Richards, Davis, Lewis, Maisano, and Seibold 1994). But many of the conclusions derive from my reflections in the two years since the team disbanded, and for these I take sole responsibility. Hindsight continues to clarify for me the processes of transition we experienced.

THE PROJECT

This is a report from a three-year project that is still ongoing (and may never end!). Funded 1991-1993 by the National Health and Medical Research Council of Australia, and Victorian Health Promotions Foundation, its mission was to study menopause and mid-life as a social construction rather than a medical event. We were to gather data over three years on all aspects of the social construction of menopause. Our design incorporated qualitative and feminist methodologies, and required combining qualitative and quantitative data from a wide variety of sources. Data was to include unstructured accounts in individual and group interviews of highly personal experiences by women experiencing menopause. Some of these accounts were to be longitudinal with reinterviews after a year and diaries kept by the women. We were also to report on the knowledge women accessed from professional advisers and make reviews of the popular media. Detailed analysis of all of these sources on women's experiences of managing the change of life and having it managed for them was to include the family, work, and social contexts within which they do this, and the knowledge and authority structures involved. The grant body further required that we combine qualitative and quantitative approaches, conducting a large-scale survey of women.

These requirements of large-scale, extremely varied data were set against commitment to traditional approaches to theory construction and theme discovery that are normally applied to small-scale data. The project was originally designed to provide rich records from group and individual interviews, and the grant application showed a strong emphasis on "grounded theory" techniques of open coding and theoretical sampling (Strauss 1987). But we clearly felt we were working in a context of challenges to qualitative method.

> For ethical, practical and political reasons it was important that data management also be rigorous. We wanted to be sure the contributions of those talking to us were not wasted, processing was consistent and detailed accounts of our methods of handling data and ways of arriving at categories and linking them in theories were kept. The project is set in a highly contentious debate, and one in which "positivist" "biomedical" thinking has been much attacked. In health research, qualitative work, especially feminist qualitative work, remains suspect. If we were to be listened to, we needed reportable and replicable processes of data management and analysis (Richards and Simon 1993).

THE SOFTWARE

The project was proposed, with great confidence, as a NUD•IST project, (software for Non-Numerical Unstructured Data Indexing Searching and Theorizing).[1] For the first two years we used version 2.3 of the software, transferring in the third year to the then new version 3.0. This paper cannot offer "objective" evaluation of the software package since the author is co-developer of the software. Indeed, the experiences reported here contributed substantially to the design of the next versions of the software. (For objective evaluation of NUD•IST, and comparisons with other qualitative computing software, see Weitzman and Miles 1995, Chapter 6; for other detailed accounts see Richards and Richards 1991a, 1994b.) The present paper offers an account of experience in a project designed with knowledge of what the software could then do, and the sort of critical reflection that developer-users can possibly best offer. (Like mothers, we are often the toughest critics of our offsprings' performance!)

The software supports a range of ways of handling data, some extending traditional methods, some offering new approaches. Most traditional methods for handling qualitative data rely on some process of coding documents. Text is then retrieved via coding. The method has serious problems, (Richards and Richards

1994b), but is nevertheless essential to much qualitative research, and supported by all qualitative computing software. NUD•IST does both coding and retrieving in ways designed for flexibility and exploratory freedom. Data and ideas are organized in separate document and index systems, so that the conceptual structure can be built up and explored through and independent of data records. The data documents remain "clean" of coding; to code a segment of a document, the researcher puts a reference to that segment at the "node" in the index system where the required category is located. NUD•IST allows data documents to be either online (typed into any word processor) or off-line (stored somewhere else). The program can index any off-line document it is told of, (by entering references to any appropriate units such as page numbers or tape count numbers, etc.) though of course it cannot retrieve or search text that is not typed into the computer.

The index system provides a flexible container for categories, their definitions, and ideas in memos about them as well as coding or indexing of documents at them. Any or all of these sorts of information can be stored at *nodes*, which the researcher creates, deletes, shifts, and reorganizes. Nodes can be kept in a simple list, or organized in index "trees," hierarchies of category, subcategory, sub-sub-category, and so forth. Like a library index, this assists the researcher to locate and recall the structure of categories, but unlike the library index it invites change, and stores not only locations but ideas, facts (about respondents, situations, etc.), and the research process. There is effectively no restriction, except the limitations of the hardware, on either the number of categories created or the number of times references to text can be put at nodes in the index system, or changes to coding or the locations, definitions, and ideas about categories. This makes it possible for coding to be combined with other analytical work, exploration of text, memo writing, searching for patterns, in the interplay of the conceptual index with the documents from which categories are developed, and regrouping and recoding as understanding grows.

These features are central to the reputation of the software, and of course informed our research design. We *knew* what objective reviewers later reported: "NUD•IST's firm but flexible hierarchical structure, along with the ability to reorganize and 'collect' and 'inherit' are superb" (Weitzman and Miles 1995, p. 256). For researchers, the software thus promises and encourages removal of constraint. Even if used only for coding, it means that coding potentially becomes less a clerical than a theorizing task, with emphasis on fluidity and growth of both text and index databases and their interaction.

Analysis tools can search either the text of documents or the patterns of indexing at nodes. Text can be searched for strings or patterns of characters (find all the places that "sick" or "ill" or "unwell" were used in these discussions). The index system can be searched using Boolean (and/or/not) searches (to ask, for instance, what text is indexed at "trust of doctors" *and* "acceptance of hormone treatments"). Or more subtle searches can be conducted, concerned with ordering, sequence, or context of coding ("give me all of the text about accepting these treatments if later in the document the woman told us she trusted the doctor"). Results of such searches can be automatically coded, so another question can be asked: *which* women said this, and what if anything did those women say about "alternative" treatments? String searching and code and retrieve techniques can be combined in asking more questions (did these women use the words "sick", "ill," or "unwell"). Weitzman and Miles say of index searching, "This is where NUD•IST has all the others beat, hands down" (1995, p. 248). Given such tools, your ability to integrate data will be restricted only by the adequacy of your codes and coding.

The tools are also designed explicitly for theory discovery and construction. A main feature of NUD•IST, designed for theory building, is that discoveries should be returned to the index system as more data in processes termed "system closure" (Richards and Richards 1994b; Weitzman and Miles 1995). The results of either a text search or an index system search can be saved as more indexing, either as a new node or merged with the indexing at an existing node. This feature is how "automatic coding" is done by text search; when the required string of characters is found, the researcher can specify the part of the document to be indexed, and the node at which this is done. But it was designed primarily to support theory construction. The ability to save the results of searches means they can be part of further questioning. Since the results of text or index searches can be put back as more data, at existing or new categories, these can in turn be explored in combinations with other categories, allowing the researcher to build on and interrogate the results of past analyses, express and test hypotheses in processes of iterative theory-building and theory-testing.

As a set, then, the software's tools offer seductive invitations to go where manual methods could not go. They also offer to get the researcher there very quickly, with command files automating all processes. None of these directions is *required* by the software. But our experience showed the difficulty of resisting the removal of constraints and possibilities of exploration. To summarize, in three methodological areas, previous constraints are effectively removed.

1. *Data: The challenge of variety and volume.* NUD•IST does not require mixed or massive data records. (My own favorite projects are very integrated and their document systems are small.) But the software places effectively no restriction on the varieties or volumes of documents.

    - The only restriction to size and number of documents is time and the size of the hard disk.
    - Online data can be indexed along with data that is not typed on, breaking the dependence on data the computer can contain, and reopening the method to less cut and dried data.
    - Off-line documents can be anything the researcher can "tell" the computer about: large printed documents or reports, photographs, tapes or handwritten records, and so forth.
    - Any amount of information about people, cases, situations, and so forth, whether it applies to whole documents or any part of documents, can be stored in the index system.
    - Quantitative records can be linked with qualitative ones by expressing the values of variables in the nodes of the hierarchical index system.

2. *Coding: The challenge of not having to stop.* NUD•IST does not require that the researcher ever code anything; indeed a project can have no index system, or can have a very small or completely unchanging one. But should the researcher wish to code data, the software offers no barriers.

   - The index system can be as large and as complex as the data and emerging theory requires, categories can be organized in infinitely flexible structures of category, subcategories, and so forth.
   - There is effectively no restriction on the richness of coding of documents. Text can be coded as many times as its meanings require.
   - Flexibility is also unlimited: categories created for coding can be expanded, altered, combined, or deleted at will.
   - Memos can be edited as much as needed, keeping a full audit trail of development of ideas, definitions, and changing understandings of codes.

3. *Theorizing: The challenge of flexibility.* NUD•IST can be used simply for retrievals by single topics (just make an editable report, with the text, on the indexing at a node). But should the researcher wish to go further, there is a wide range of ways of combining the processes of interrogation of data by text or index system searching. "NUD•IST has by far the most extensive and powerful set of code-based retrieval operators around" (Weitzman and Miles 1995, p. 248).

   - Rapid retrievals and ability to store them for further questioning mean it is easy to ask an "I wonder whether" question, store the answer, and ask another.
   - Ideas can be developed and altered in an index *system*, recording and using the relationships of category and subcategory and designing clearly coordinated indices.
   - Revision of existing categories and recoding of text means researchers are able to respond when new categories or interpretations emerge.

- Memos can be written and edited (forever!) to record and assist thinking about documents or categories and their relationships.
- Ideas, memos, and data extracts can be moved between parts of the project and into reports (the software has its own editor), and memos can be introduced and coded as a data document.

Hence the program offers (though of course it does not require) ways researchers can manage effectively unlimited and varied data records, with very sensitive data input and exploration processes. With a fast user interface, it invites the researcher to try these. Where your software has "unparalleled power" (Weitzman and Miles 1995, p. 248) it is hard to resist the offer. The set of tools can be used in very simple projects for very small, detailed investigations. But it also can support larger and more complex investigations. For those it offers many ways of never finishing your study!

The story below is about the effects of this overwhelming invitation. The research experience was transformed by the use of this computer software. It was not always a comfortable transformation, but in each area where we met challenges we also developed new strategies.

UNLIMITED DATA?

Size Limits

In the context of a large and complex project, removing constraints on size had immediate results. Bulk data could get bulkier as the challenging topic was tackled, and there were seemingly endless possibilities for expanding our data and pursuing other lines of enquiry. We learned fast that the size of a hard disk is not an adequate boundary to data collection. More important, the ability of the computer to swallow any number of documents at any time at first was very confusing.

Strategy?

Slowly we learned to monitor data accrual by using the index system. By creating nodes for different types of data, and indexing documents at them, we could use NUD•IST's searchers to monitor for us the polyglot records we were creating. Its tools for pattern-investigating (especially, in version 3.0, matrix and vector) could display the data by type, (so we could find if nurses in different professional settings, for instance, were giving different sorts of advice.) We could then keep track of data acquisition, select limits to records, and do informed theoretical sampling.

Varieties of Data

The research design required a substantial body of data with very many different sorts of records, and the software encouraged us to maximize variety. By the third year we had recognized the problem.

> We made the mistake of accruing data if we might need it, invited by the memory space of the computer. In the first year, we committed to the computer vast quantities of text we never want to see or use again, and learned the hard way that total text retention is neither necessary nor desirable for qualitative projects. Many records, e.g., notes from telephone interviews, contained little material whose verbatim text we wanted to examine. Coding of documents could record the fact that a topic was discussed, or a person mentioned. Online text was essential only for text search (Richards and Simon 1993).

This was despite a proliferation of documents that resisted typing on. Field research in the second and third year produced handwritten notes; women in one sector kept diaries.

> Obvious candidates for off-line documents! But that proved a hard decision. At first we decided to leave out of the computer documents that were clearly expensive to transcribe or difficult to scan (e.g., magazine articles and newspaper cuttings). But we begrudged the loss of text as we learnt to use the software's ability to retrieve (in an editable report) exactly

the text segments we wanted to think about more, and to use text search for automatic coding (Richards and Simon 1993).

Strategy?

We devised a useful compromise: the online summary of an offline document, containing code-words which could be located for automatic coding, and transcriptions of parts of the text we might wish to study further. When budgets or hard disk space or time are limited, such a summary combines what are usually three stages of research, since the same person is reading and summarising the article online, and recording coding decisions. Text of the summary can be searched to locate quotations, or to do automatic coding by searching for the code-words typed in. Our magazine article summaries were brief and groups of them could be put into large documents, the individual articles marked as sections for auto-coding in NUD•IST. The program could then search for the required word, and on finding it code the section at the required node (Richards and Simon 1993).

Quantitative and Qualitative?

Part of the research design was to link quantitative and qualitative records, and there was a particular interest in exploring possibilities of convergence of survey and qualitative methods. The funding bodies had required a bulk of survey data which could never have been handled by traditional qualitative methods. However the software would permit detailed coding and linking of qualitative and quantitative records, by command files.

We approached the survey with appalling confidence! I expressed my faith in the software by addressing the ethical problems of surveying in sensitive areas with a custom-designed schedule whose format invited open-ended answers. All too successful, this approach won 1,069 open-ended interviews; women wrote in the spaces provided, on the back, on added paper! We devised commands to "tell" NUD•IST everything the statistical package "knew" about each of the 1,069 women. The task is logically simple, since NUD•IST can store information about the values of variables in the form of coding at nodes. For each node representing a precoded question, the subnodes can represent the possible answers.

It Seemed a Good Strategy...?

We did it on a large scale. A whole tree of nodes was created (by command file, of course), with a node for each variable and subnodes for each value. By coding the document at a subnode, we could "tell" NUD•IST this was the answer given in that document to that question. Then using the index system searchers we could ask for all the text in other parts of the document on a topic if the document answered that question in a certain way, or the respondent had certain characteristics. Data entry could be done in such a way that one block of typing could go into both quantitative and qualitative programs. When the survey data was typed up for the statistical package (in this case SPSSX), open-ended answers were entered as memo fields. The same input typing could produce text that could be read by both the statistical package and NUD•IST. A command file told NUD•IST to do automatic coding of each variable by text search for each value of it. (In the years since, other researchers have produced variants of this strategy. Exactly the same auto-coding process can be used by inserting into the document the output from a stats package describing that case. Or the input or output document can simply be edited to make it a command file that will do the coding.)

This formidable process produced uniquely linked statistical and qualitative databases and satisfying "Wow" comments from observers. But the price was high. Weeks of time taken with clerical tasks resulted in a massive index system. The lessons learned were serious.

Warnings!

The command files were large (76 pages), and while they are very simple to write, the repetitious commands they contain require very careful checking. Errors went through undetected, discovered only when the task was completed.

The attainment of mass coding of all this factual information also offered another challenge. Qualitative data, given such formidable contexting information, is hard to handle qualitatively. This is not the software's "fault" or the designers' intention—the researcher can resist the temptation to use such a wealth of information. But in later stages we found that, since so much factual information was available, it was hard to resist and the research process slipped into a sort of quasi-variable analysis. It was easier to ask questions about whether the answers patterned on age group or medical history than to try to tease out the meanings of in vivo codes. That is fine if that is the research process required, but we had set out to construct theory from exploration of meanings in the data, not to test for patterning on demographic variables.

These warnings apply to any process of storage of considerable factual information, whether or not it is done in conjunction with a stats package. And the strategic discoveries we made are all about over-coding.

CODING: THE CHALLENGE OF NOT HAVING TO STOP

Most researchers would agree that qualitative coding should be aimed at discovering, recording, and exploring new ideas and surprises. But most would also admit that coding easily becomes routine and boring. Coding, or putting references to documents at nodes, in NUD•IST can serve creative purposes or do purely descriptive information storage. Exploration of text, on the screen, can be exciting and theory-productive. But our experience was that we had to fight the temptation to do endless coding that was merely descriptive, or "mundane" (Miles and Huberman 1994).

Descriptive Coding: Did I Want to Know That?

Most researchers have to do some such mundane coding, and most dread it. It kills the excitement in the data; you forget what she looked like when she said that. ... The challenge is to make mundane coding as rapid and automatic as possible, leaving the researcher to concentrate on the exciting tasks of coding that contribute to thinking and theorizing.

The present project made that challenge much greater because so much purely descriptive coding was being done. The varieties of data described above seemed to demand vast amounts of factual coding. That challenge of storing factual data clearly becomes greater as the task is enlarged, no matter how efficient the technique is made. Efficiency contributes to the problem: without the software's command files we would never had considered doing the factual coding of the survey in NUD•IST. Thus ironically the task was enlarged formidably by the power of the computer.

So why not cut down on the information stored? The problem is that since qualitative method seeks surprises, explores the unexpected, it is hard to guess what might be useful in that exploration, *which* mundane coding might we want access to when we were further into exploring these documents? How do you know what to store in advance? You cannot, since qualitative method is about discovering what you want to know. In the first year, we suffered a sort of fetishism of storing everything we knew. In the years since, only a tiny proportion of this coding was used.

Strategy!

The solution is so obvious that I wince when I report it. Belatedly, we realized that our need to store information about respondents did not require that all that coding be done in advance. If those things you know about the person are *in the text,* NUD•IST can find them by text search and index the appropriate parts of a document. No need to create the nodes for that information until they are needed: they can be created, and the coding done, at any time. We needed only to insert in the document keywords that will not occur in normal text. (If that information is coming from a statistics package, the variable names and values are probably mnemonics; if the information is being inserted in documents by the researcher, simply use a character to ensure the descriptors are not words that will occur elsewhere (e.g., "% female; % full-time work").

Perhaps that theme of women's working at transitions is related to their work force participation? Send NUD•IST to search for "% full-time work," save at a new node each interview where it found that string. Ask your question by an index system search, save that answer too if you want to ask another, but delete all these working nodes when the line of enquiry is completed.

My conclusion now is that the possibility of storing a lot of variable information about people or documents should almost always be approached with great caution. It was all too easy to store information which we were evidently unlikely to use. A large index system slows the computer. Perhaps more importantly, it distorts the picture of the project, by loading it with nodes that are merely information carriers. Routinization of the coding became a main threat in our project. We had to keep reminding ourselves that coding is not merely a chore, but the crucial interface between data, knowledge about data records, and ideas.

The final solution was to *delete!* all the nodes created by the monster command files, and revert to working simply with the text of the documents, which includes the text of the SPSS input. Whenever I wish to know what SPSS "knows" about the women, NUD•IST can do the search for me.

Coding for Theorizing

What of the interactive coding that is the researcher's way of storing meanings seen in text—what were we really trying to do? Here, the first experiences with the software are entirely of relief and excitement. Compared with manual or most computer methods, coding in NUD•IST is far easier, and far less trammeled by restrictions on variety and fluidity of discovered meanings. This is especially true of the graphical user interface version that we upgraded to in the project's third year. You can get high on coding! The text is on the screen, you have only to highlight text and press a key and the software asks where you want to code the marked passage. It is done in an instant, and you are returned to the highlighted passage to wonder what else it is about. If you had no node for that category, it is created and the coding done at it, and the text returns inviting another thought. You can have on the screen the memos storing ideas about this person or event, the category you are wondering about and the material already coded at it, you can copy quotations from reports into the memo, then return to wonder again about that highlighted text.

Thus, far *more* coding can be done in far *more* categories. (The usual story; NUD•IST *requires* nothing, but invites a lot.) Any text can be coded *as richly* as it deserves. If data builds up and coding is delayed, the task starts to look rather as a very large wave does when you and a small surfboard are immediately below it.

Putting It Off: The Problems of Delaying Coding

> We delayed. This was not part of the research design, rather a combination of awe at the richness of our data, and the onset of serious workload problems. The momentum of snowball sampling made it impossible to delay the growth in data records. But the time to examine and explore the records, and index their contents was always hard to find (Richards and Simon 1993).

Strategy

We learned after the event that starting coding, and keeping it alongside the making of more data, would have helped enormously. After the event, it became evident that part of our problem was a feeling that each document should be *done*, coded in all required ways, in turn. (Legacy of survey training? Or of the coding-is-a-chore memories of manual methods?) Coding in a filing cabinet, or on index cards, is too time consuming for the researcher to entertain the possibility of returning to rethink, recode, as qualitative methods require.

But revisiting data is swift and easy in NUD•IST so there is no need to "do" a document in one coding session. By the final year of the project, we had learned to address some of the terror of coding by a first pass through data, doing descriptive coding and recording first impressions, locating generic themes, and storing early ideas, then returning to them later. The first-pass work can be rapid, using the computer to do automated coding.

Descriptive coding can be done by text search for keywords. Auto-coding can be used for some theme indexing. NUD•IST could search for "HRT" or "hormone replacement therapy," or "estrogen" (spelled lots of ways!) and auto-index all the answers to questions in which these were mentioned, to give us access to all the data on this topic before the detailed coding was done. Once this first-pass coding is done, the researcher has access to the data to explore, reflect on it.

We exploited first-pass coding, however, only as a means of monitoring of data.

> The patterns of data on crucial demographic or context variables can be easily viewed and the way the sample is panning out can be reviewed and patterns of answers explored *early*. Further sampling can be informed by systematic exploration of the data using index system searches (do the women who are full-time employed have different attitudes to the promises of "HRT" to alleviate symptoms of menopause?) (Richards and Simon 1993).

Later, working in other projects, I realized "open coding" work can be done in a novel and very productive way, using retrievals on this first-pass coding. The ability to retrieve by topic allows "fracturing" of the data, juxtaposing the different comments and allowing discovery of patterns, giving a new "cut" on it to locate recurrent themes, surprising ideas (Strauss 1987).

Coding and Confidence

Confronted with the problems of coding delay, most of us felt uncertainty and diffidence in the face of our very rich data and the software's capabilities. What had seemed, using manual methods, like a relatively minor data-processing task (as indeed it is in numerical coding) much more clearly presented now as a central analytical one. Looking back, I realize the software revealed how *theorizing* is the coding process. The coder constantly makes theoretical decisions about what will be a category, what text is to be coded in that category, how it should be defined, and where it goes in the overall picture. In NUD•IST, these decisions were clarified and their results visible and open to exploration. As with most qualitative research, the terror is in actually claiming to have a theory.

So how to deal with diffidence? All coding starts diffident. We needed strategies to take the terror out of category creation and coding decisions, and to encourage exploratory, "I wonder whether…?" coding. Such coding had to be seen as clearly tentative, not part of a rigid index system, but the researcher also had to be confident it would not be wasted.

Strategy

Ability to structure an index hierarchically and manipulate it by shifting nodes around became precious. With confidence, much more casual approaches to the index system were developed. This particularly meant rethinking our relationship to the hierarchical organizing of nodes, and recognizing that while the software did not require hierarchy, we were assuming it.

> There is an unusual twist, and theoretical implication, to the tree structure of NUD•IST's index system: it works from the top down. In most research paradigms, you begin at the level of the data … you build your way up from the data to first-level codes, second-level codes, and so on (Weitzman and Miles 1995, p. 252).

Right: you have to be able to begin at the "first-level" and work up, gathering nodes together under a higher-level category only when this is appropriate. The following ways of thinking and working proved invaluable.

- All categories start unconnected, and it proves useful to think of them as unconnected until/unless they clearly come to "belong" somewhere. We learned to create nodes freely whenever a possibly interesting category occurred. If it is, as one inspired punster remarked, node-worthy, give it a node. It can always be deleted later if it proves uninteresting.
- It helps considerably to think of the index system as safe housing for categories rather than a rigid map or model of

the project's theory. If categories are created "bottom-up" from the data during coding, they can be collected unconnected in the index system, ideas stored at them, and the coding links to the documents will be safely held until shifted, explored, or deleted.

- As apparently unconnected categories occur, they can be "parked" in the index system under "working" nodes, later shifted to another part of the index system. We realized we had been far too keen to make these "belong" in a tidy system. Shades of the filing cabinet! NUD•IST did not mind if they never were linked to other categories.
- We invented ways with "working nodes" that give a sense of easy use of the index:

  * each researcher has a "working" node for their current wild ideas: instant agenda for the team meeting
  * a Monday node, Tuesday node, and so forth, for all of that day's ideas and discoveries—if Monday comes round again it is time to tidy up those nodes!

- We learned to gather at a generic category references to text not yet finely understood, so we could later retrieve, explore, use grounded theory techniques on the broad picture. Thus, for example, rather than have separate categories for positive and negative responses to a treatment, by coding at a node for *any* attitudes to it we could avoid preemptive dichotomizing of what might be subtly different responses. Tentative coding at broadly defined categories can later be retrieved and more finely subcategorized.
- Researchers working "up" out of the data can create an assortment of idiosyncratic, finely distinguished categories (often coding only one document). Later, as they get more confidence in what the data is saying, they can use the ability of NUD•IST to "collect" all data coded at subcategories of a node and present it for recoding.
- Ideas about these tentative, guess-work codings can be stored at node memos, which can be time-stamped and followed up when return to the data is possible.

- We discovered also that qualitative computing highlights issues of the aesthetics of qualitative analysis, and we were helped by attending to these. Our software offered a range of ways of doing most things, and we found different styles were encouraged. Once coding began in earnest, team members doing it developed very different preferred techniques. Some "still" printed out documents and scribbled on them. Some discovered they preferred ways of coding on computer, using command files, rather than marking up paper copies of documents and later transferring the coding to NUD•IST. The preference was an interesting example of the differences in researcher style. (There was a negative correlation in our research team between seniority and willingness to index with command files! It is very easy to create a command file template to "Add-indexing," simply by editing a list of all nodes. But command file indexing saves time at the price of dependency on a computer, and routinization of work.)
- We learned to exploit windows interfaces by making coding always part of many other tasks. To have a memo (or six) up on the screen at the same time helped the researcher to flit between the recognition of a category in text and the exploration of an idea therein (Richards, Davis et al. 1994).

THEORIZING: THE CHALLENGE OF FLEXIBILITY

Coding in NUD•IST thus immediately seemed endless. This is not because it is harder than by manual methods. On the contrary, it is just because the process becomes swift and simple. With no limits to the number of categories or the number of times that very rich data could be indexed, so much more could be done. The challenge then is to balance this increased load by supporting swifter coding and creative work. On reflection, I think this is another way in which the computer exposes methodological features that were always there, but less evident. The tendency especially when you are tired is to slip into "if it moves, code it" mode.

Using the Index System

The major threat was that organization seemed constantly to take over from creativity. We knew the software would support playful, exploratory research, storing of fly-by-night, intuitive, imaginative ideas, building up tentative theories and chasing them through data, rigorously testing them, sensitively exploring their relation to other ideas. But for months we seemed to do none of that.

> Partly, it seemed, this was because the task of adding indexing has such a momentum that anyone doing it found their concentration broken if they took time "out" to type up their reflections. More significantly, it was because an observation or insight often seemed obvious or trivial, perhaps worth scribbling in a notebook, but hardly worth a new comment in the index system that all researchers could view (Richards and Simon 1993).

For example, we discovered that each of us in different ways had been observing what I came to call "transition work," but none had seen the *work* side of transitions as deserving a memo. For at least some members of the team, it was harder to commit these scruffy hunches to computer than to scribble them down. But this is the stuff qualitative researchers' theories get built from, "little things that relate in some meaningful way":

> And so the web—of code, explore, relate, study the text grows, resulting in little explorations, little tests, little ideas hardly worth calling theories (Richards and Richards 1994, p. 448).

Keeping Ideas Moving

How to keep producing the new ideas, the surprises, the insights, and importantly, the changes in understanding, that come from detailed knowledge of the data? Our experience in this regard strongly influenced design of the next version (3.0) of the software.

Strategies

- Collaborative ideas can be created, stored, debated, and nodes and records can be kept of changing definitions.

Listing the nodes allows discussion of the emerging shape of index.

- Ideas at memos should be stored much more often, much more freely, in teams, initialized by author, edited to include the text from which the idea sprang, that we think we understand or still need to explore.
- By using and maintaining the log trail of changing ideas, date stamping memos, noting changes of definition, the researcher can monitor and report analysis processes (Singh forthcoming).
- Our experience with memos, when they were started, was that they often grew into small essays or segments of analysis, documents in their own right, to be expanded into discussion papers, covering many topics. These can be copied and saved as documents for coding at all relevant nodes in the index system. And the processes learned from grounded theory can be explored and ideas derived from them recorded. What is it to "put things on hold"? Under what conditions does one do so? Compare with the power of a telephonist, who can prevent you communicating...

Making an Index that Works

Dominated by the growing bulk of data, we took a long time to begin constructing an index system, beyond the nodes that represented questions being asked or information about people, cases, institutions, and so forth that we needed to store. Once we started creating and organizing conceptual categories, the process seemed of heroic dimensions:

> Working with a first body of interviews with professionals, we dealt the categories into manageable piles, at first simply distinguishing sets of ideas. First attempts to index a few documents proved new categories were generated at an alarming rate. Gathered and ordered on the computer, they were worked over until we were able to add to or reshape the index system with confidence, and see patterns much more clearly. This stage brought with it a burst of discovery and exploration of new aspects of the project, as we shaped trees and discussed other logical possibilities, nodes we should logically have but which the data so far had not required. The

system was changing with every document indexed, but changes almost always could be assimilated in the broad structure, and categories existed for most of the data we were collecting. At last it was possible to see the shapes of the accruing data.

A second period of instability occurred when a new project stage brought data from mid-life women to challenge categories developed from data from nurses and other professionals. The index system now showed its bias to professional concerns, and we learnt to note as interesting the absence of a node in a logical structure. For instance, the Ideas tree had branches for ideas about mid-life women held by professionals, but none for public images of mid-life women, such as media portrayals of the superwoman image, a matter of major concern to women, but apparently not to professionals.

This second round of redesign of the index system was not only much easier but also very productive of ideas. On the basis of interviewing grass roots professionals, categories about treatments had been organized in one tree. As we gathered data about other advice and suggestions, in the women's interviews, from marriage guidance to t'ai chi, we recognized that these "belonged" with medical treatments in a wider category of strategies discussed by women and their advisers in dealing with the issues of menopause. At this stage, the redesign task became both simple and enjoyable. NUD•IST's support for reshaping and shifting of index trees meant there was no need to pull apart the whole system, and no need to waste any of the work so far.

These lessons were learned too late to save not only time but also anxiety.

We learnt very quickly that the ability of the software to support flexibility and change did not automatically equip its human users with ability to stand too much of this! Especially in a team project, rigidity always seemed safer. We slowly learned that not all of an index system had to be developed at the start, and there was no need to agree on very much, so long as we kept a record of what we were thinking. We decided to wait until a portion of data from each section of the project had been indexed before we developed that part of the system.

There were problems, however, in this "staging." During team meetings, we would discuss a new category and then discover a tendency of all or some members of the team to begin to see this theme everywhere, possibly at the expense of others. A sudden fascination with women going to pharmacists for help turned out to have come from only two cases! We developed ways of interrogating such themes, talking with others who were coding, searching for occurrences and exploring their patterns and keeping memos about the processes. A storage space for such possibilities was needed, as by their charismatic nature they often did not fit anywhere; we developed a tree of "Working nodes" to park these ideas whilst they were developing (Richards and Simon 1993).

Strategies

- From this long process we concluded that index construction should not be allowed to appear as threatening or become too time-consuming. Nor should it become the (dangerously power-related) province of one or a few team members.
- My recommendation now, having learned the hard way, is: Go straight onto the computer! If the NUD•IST project is started when the grant application or literature review is commenced it provides a container for all the early contributions, literature review, notes, and so forth. Rather as the nervous thesis writer learns the advantage of putting the first draft onto the word processor, we learned that the index system can begin and be shaped in NUD•IST, with no work wasted as reshaping happens.
- We learned to use the graphical display of the index shape, and the numerical record of the location of nodes, to map an index and move confidently around it.
- NUD•IST offers to record the life history of a node. It took a while to realize the potential of this record of dates and changes for showing us where we were and where we had been, and for providing an account that could be cited in reports, explaining the origin and emergence of a category and the ways it had been explored through the data. The lesson we learned was to use this audit trail early.
- Ability to do continual reindexing, reshaping of the categories, and recording of ideas about them and their links, and building on answers and discoveries to ask further questions threatens to create an ever-extending process of data management. None of this was *required* by the software: it merely makes it possible. So we could not *blame* the computer, yet we often felt that somehow we were its

victims. As the project progressed, we learned to adapt the tool kit offered by the software, in ways that gave more of a sense of ownership of the research design and control over our enquiry processes.

- Ability to enquire, to explore, to play with ideas about the data, became more enjoyable as we simplified the index system and strengthened our knowledge of the data, using open coding procedures and storing the emerging ideas in memos at nodes.
- No index system is perfect, so don't try! We produced a set of rules for non-perfect workable systems.

1. Start an index system as soon as categories are known (but be aware of the possible biases in the data that first generates categories).
2. Keep like categories together. As with any taxonomic system, clarity of the principles on which categories are grouped will help recall and stimulate new ideas about further categories. It will also allow maximal exploitation of features in NUD•IST, especially the ability of the software to "collect" all indexing references at the subcategories below a node, or "inherit" indexing at nodes above.
3. Keep unlike categories apart. To conflate different sorts of categories is to risk losing all the benefits of hierarchical organization and confusing the meanings of categories.
4. It is usually helpful to keep the index system theoretically innocent. Rather than build into the system assumptions about what will be found, it is preferable to create the categories with which you can ask questions of the data.
5. Index systems are best designed collaboratively: discuss it, draw it up, display and debate it. There were many times, when weighed down by the seemingly endless task of coding, we became, in a sense, too close to the growing index.
6. Keep it simple and elegant. We learned late to trust the tools NUD•IST provides for pruning, shifting, and reviewing the index system and its contents.
7. But that would break our seventh rule—know when to stop. It is necessary to stop changing the basic structure in order to provide the confidence and familiarity that will support thorough exploration, theory construction, rapid and tentative questioning, and detailed, rigorous testing of theory.

When can this be done? The project rapidly established the basic rule that you can ask in NUD•IST almost anything that can be expressed in terms of the nodes in the index system. So our conclusion was that the process of index construction could stop when the index system either had the nodes to ask the questions for which answers were required, or had the nodes to build them (Richards and Simon 1993). These are, of course, not rigid rules, and many other guidelines apply (set out in detail in the software's manuel).

Exploring and Theorizing

This paper has concentrated on the stages of early data processing—for a good reason. Once those stages and the attendant challenges were overcome, analysis happened. Searching of text of online documents, and searching of the index system to ask questions about the patterns of coding, were combined increasingly in excursions into the data. Text search was used to discover occurrences of words or phrases or parts of them, or any pattern defined by special characters, to catch occurrences of in vivo codes, or trace a theme through people's accounts. Index system searches became increasingly playful and productive, using that range of operators which we knew were "the program's forte" (Weitzman and Miles 1995, p. 256). We learned to use these to make new cuts of the data for open coding, offering all the material on a combination of topics, so we could read and discuss it; see it anew. We began to enjoy the instant access to data by patterning operators. Using NUD•IST, we could obtain in seconds a qualitative matrix, cutting the data by age groups, for instance, or attitudes to health professionals. A set of such matrices offered the basis for very confident—and startling—analysis.

Enjoyment of these processes entirely altered our feelings for the data, and we regretted delaying the playing with data this way. The strictures of all methods teachers to their students to start thinking about the data early have, we concluded, a double meaning in computed projects. We had been *thinking* from the start, the thinking expressed in categories and ideas stored at them. But we delayed *playing*, the delicate, iterative explorations of emerging theory that nudge understanding forward. The software supports such play from the moment that text is introduced (look for words, ask who is saying them...) and categories created (what does this category have to do with that one?) The ability of the computer to support pursuit of hunches and odd noises in the data is as essential as its formidable ability to support theory-testing. My advice to other researchers now stresses enjoyment over organization.

Strategies

- Plan playing. It took a while to recognize that the software would not stop us playing with the data forever. Unlike a project being handled manually, this one had to set its own stopping points and analytical end points, rather than rely on being stopped by data handling limits. The program allows constant additions to or subtractions from the index system, modification and recoding at any stage in a project. It is also possible to do infinitely thorough and multiple coding. This means a rethinking of the strictly sequential process of normal data gathering and coding. The ability to carry analysis and interrogation of emerging themes ever further upward in the creation of new index categories means a new pressure to recognize, and possibly even to formalize, the point at which this becomes counterproductive.
- Expand the techniques of grounded theory, both to support the text-book processes of open coding and memo recording, and to offer ways of enhancing those processes. Grounded theory traditionally does not rely on, even does not use, the code-and-retrieve methods most often supported by computer programs (Strauss 1987). We found the tools most relevant in NUD•IST were not its coding processes, but the processes of category construction and manipulation and storage of ideas.

  * Storage of codes as they emerged, at nodes in the index system, was done with storage of definitions and frequently edited memos.
  * Nodes created as codes were discovered in the data, were explored by manipulation of the index system so the

relation between nodes could be investigated. Gathering of nodes was used to express dimensions of a code or its subcategories.

Thus, as transition processes were explored, the category of "transition work" was created, and grew, as we gathered and compared the accounts women gave of working at the transitions of mid-life. Nodes were created below "transition work" to hold in vivo codes ("putting things on hold," "time out") and our growing ideas about what these expressed.

- Exploit the ability to explore relations of codes in the data, developing the category using the flexible ways of asking questions by index system search. Which women talked about "putting things on hold?" What did their family history have to do with this? If the theme recurred, we worked with systematic comparisons through the data, grounding the emerging theory not only in future instances but in the retrieved record of accounts already explored.
- Be inventive! As our confidence in the computer's ability to support play with data grew, we invented new ways of getting new "cuts" on the data, for exploring an intriguing theme, or simply for seeing the data anew. (One very fruitful trick was to copy into a new temporary node references to any text that could throw some light on an aspect of the data, search for related words, and copy the results into the "bucket." Also copy any nodes about related themes. NUD•IST merges those references and will give all the text to which they refer, in a new sampling of data that always surprises.)
- Never underestimate text search. It is a blunt instrument for theme identification, but powerful not only for identifying the occurrence of words or phrases but also for searching for related ideas. Using pattern matching text searches we could locate these throughout the data and automatically index them, so their occurrence could be explored and documented. Being able to return to the text

in which they had occurred, or ask the computer to give a wider context of a quotation, made it possible to move between the isolated concept and the context.

- Always ask another question! System closure provides for combining text and index system searching to build new nodes from answers to questions. Theory construction and exploration can be done by iteratively building new ideas on old. Having asked which women are saying this, we could chase the other ideas in their accounts, finding which codes cohered, and where. The move toward discovery of "core categories" requires such explorations and is assisted by the computer's fine fingertip access to data. Links can be expressed as hypotheses and tested by index system search (was it only the women in full-time career occupations...?)
- Keep ideas flowing! We found entirely new ability to store results of open coding, growing ideas, understandings that grow during line-by-line analysis; ability to move ideas between memos and into documents reporting or exploring the project's amassing theory.

Doing It Together: A Note on Team Research

The expanding team and increasing division of labor made it essential to keep our discoveries or often fleeting insights accessible to other researchers. We found rapidly that neither espousal of team equality nor equal access to the computer databases guaranteed equality in recording theoretical contributions. Hesitation, especially by members who had come late to the project and were in "junior" positions, proved a problem. Time pressures threatened regular team meetings. The richness of data in each sector of the project seemed sufficient to support impressions, and in the absence of organization through consistent coding, impressions took hold and could not be tested through the data.

When coding caught up speed, toward the end of the first year, this was achieved by division of labor, normally not recommended in qualitative projects. Two new team members, who could work steadily and regularly and together, took on the coding, and thereby acquired a very different picture of the data from the impressions others had gained in the field (Richards, Davis, et al. 1994).

The project faced further problems because the computer competence of team members was very uneven. For researchers who are novices with computers, hardware and ignorance about it, operating systems and other software necessary for basic computer use, can stand as serious impediments to comfortable use of the qualitative computing software. Perhaps the most serious threat of this endlessly exciting project for me was the sense that the computer hardware and my "own" software, promising arguably the best possible management of this wonderful data, stood as a barrier and a burden to my colleagues. It was a barrier which I assumed I could easily help them climb over. This assumption was wrong. Partly this is because none of us had enough time. (Familiarity with technology needs time. Teaching needs time. Teamwork needs time. Above all, immersion in a research area needs time.) Partly it was because of the scale and momentum of the project. In a smaller project, rapid access to data, swift development of ideas, would have been possible. The long stages of data collection and management kept us away from the data.

The heavy bulk of our data and the pace at which we were driven became an increasing problem for me. It was a problem quite independent of the problems some team members were having with computers. But the software made that problem worse, because it permitted bulk and pace. In retrospect, the following strategies seem obvious.

Strategies

- Prior computer competence training, independent of the project, should be offered for all members. An experienced computer user cannot take over the job of interpreting software for another researcher.
- Establish hardware and software requirements before tackling project analysis. The majority of our team's

computer problems were prior to actually using the specialist software—and often prevented the researcher from using it. Training in the particular software, for team members new to it, was the smallest problem. In each case the training had to be preceded by processes of arrival that included commitment to a research approach, exploration of topics and literatures, developing teamwork techniques. These sometimes daunting processes happened at the same time as acquiring familiarity with computers, overcoming of fear of them and dealing with hardware and software problems. It took all of us a while to realize how easy it is to attribute the problems to personal inadequacy rather than the complexity and often contradictory nature of the tangled tasks.

- Beware of divisions on computer competence, especially if they cross cut other divisions so that some team members may make others feel inadequate, or act as gatekeepers to the data.
- A team project simply cannot be treated as an extended small single-researcher project. This is especially true if it is supported by software that will allow multiple inputs from researchers and the building up and automated processing of large quantities of qualitative data. Strategies for communication, coder reliability checking and collaboration needed work. And working at these transitions, like all the other strategy work reported above, was different from the work of team projects not on computer.

CONCLUSION

The tension of creativity and organization confronts all qualitative analysis. Computers offer answers to that tension, at the price of new challenges and new tensions. These are arguably unavoidable challenges, since to dodge them by avoiding qualitative computing is to forego advantages far outweighing the problems described above. But those problems must be confronted, discussed, and strategies developed to deal with them. By the end of the project's funding, we were confidently reporting a new balance of organization and creativity.

> NUD•IST will not remove the tension of organisation and creativity. But we experience it now as a different tension. The clerical barriers between researcher and data are not removed, but they are changed, in ways that make them analytically productive. The confidence in routine data management, logging of research pathways, thorough retrievals, shifts anxiety from the ability to control the data to the ability to do it justice. With the clerical routines in place, it is easy to play in this mountain of data, feeling through and freely exploring patterns, chasing hunches and tossing around ideas. This is freedom with security: these flights of theoretical fancy are grounded in data, since at any stage, text can be put to the conceptual structure being explored, and the routes of exploration retraced. But however secure, it remains thoroughly enjoyable (Richards and Simon 1993).

Two years on, the price of the ability to create and handle bulk qualitative data is more evident. The tasks of handling so much data qualitatively defy the time available and much of the data remains unreported. My concern at the unintended consequences of computer-supported "freedom with security" grows as these issues continue to evade discussion.

A theme in the (few) published critiques of qualitative computing is that qualitative computing software programs in general, or NUD•IST in particular, are "designed to take very large data sets and organize them into readily accessible units" (Wall 1995, p. 13) and that in doing so the computer encourages analysis that is "more akin to quantitative methods." One answer, certainly, is that such distortion is the fault of (or responsibility of) the researcher.

> Although software may invoke a new potential for an infinite array of connections between previously unconnected things, we maintain that it is the researcher who must still decide what is meaningful and how it is meaningful. Moreover, the capacity to monitor and interpret one's own means of arriving at new insights—as facilitated by the "system closure" capabilities of NUDIST and other sophisticated programs—enhances the self-reflexive nature of QDA (Bassett et al. 1995, p. 18).

But while the software does not do the analysis, it is not innocent in this process of change.

> We could borrow a bromide here: "Computers don't analyze data; people do." Like its parent statement about guns, this is a half-truth. Guns do make it very easy for people to kill people. And computers make it much easier for people to think about the meaning of their data. They are not a substitute for thought, but they are a strong aid to thought (Weitzman and Miles 1995, p. 3).

Computers also make it easy for researchers to create projects that would have been unthinkable without software. No, NUD•IST was *not* designed primarily to take very large data sets, (no such software is). But certainly by making large data sets possible, and more importantly by making fingertip access to complex data sets easy, it invites such designs, when the research problem requires them (as ours did). Hence, the software irrevocably opens new methodological challenges. Once support is offered for flexibly managing data, researchers whose questions require it (and possibly some who do not, but whose methods fail to control the scale), will seek large-scale, complex, contexted multifaceted data.

To point out that NUD•IST will (and most frequently does) support tiny and simple projects, with very short time spans, does not address the problems faced by those *other* projects. The good news is that, thus supported, they can address qualitatively questions that could not previously be so addressed, with not only accuracy but also flexibility. The software supports them should they aim for theory construction and exploration, in the recording of fleeting ideas and building up of knowledge by intuitive, interactive processes.

The bad news is it will also support preemptive data reduction, automation of processes that should be preceded by reflection and quasi-quantitative analysis posing as qualitative. (Manual methods would of course support all of these undesirable outcomes!) Rresearchers resisting these possibilities will need to construct new strategies to benefit from the new powers and freedoms. They can dodge those tasks only by avoiding the potential of the software, or using simpler methods. Researchers for whom there is no acceptable option of returning to manual methods will be greatly helped by discussion of the methodological change and sharing experience of the transition and the ways it is best managed.

I owe to Cathi Lewis an informing analogy. Like our research topic, the "change of life," so too the change of methodology is both unavoidable and a social event which can easily become a personal problem. Both transitions require work. The transition must be understood, and studied, and written about, as a real structural change, socially constructed. Thus understood, and controlled, it can be an exhilarating challenge, and a productive experience. But the communication of possibilities, and sharing of solutions to problems, is essential.[2]

ACKNOWLEDGMENTS

The project grants were to myself and Jeanne Daly; the project was conducted in two parts. During the sector reported here, Dawn Simon was research assistant and the project benefited also from contributions at different times from six other women researchers, Nicole Davis, Amanda Jenkins, Cathi Lewis, Cathy Maisano, Linda Salomons, and Carmel Seibold. This account draws on observations and insights from each of them, but I take responsibility of course for its in-retrospect reflections.

NOTES

1. The NUD•IST software is developed by Qualitative Solutions and Research, P.O. Box 171, La Trobe University, Vic 3083, Australia, and distributed worldwide by Sage Publications.

2. The importance of such communication was clearly indicated when the company that markets the NUD•IST software, Qualitative Solutions and Research, recently set up its own electronic mailing list. Far from being restricted to techniques of using NUD•IST, or even to qualitative computing, it has immediately become a forum for discussions in which novice and experienced researchers from around the world take part, on a very wide range of topics about qualitative method. (Those interested in subscribing can send to qsr-forum@qsr.latrobe.edu.au, with "SUBSCRIBE" as the topic, and no message.)

REFERENCES

Bassett, R., S. Cox, and U. Rauch
1995 "The Emperor's New Clothes: Is There More to NUDIST than Meets the Eye?" *Society/Societe* 19(2)(May): 13-14.

J. Gilgun, K. Daly, and G. Handel. (Eds).
1992 *Qualitative Methods in Family Research*. Beverly Hills, CA: Sage.

Miles, M.B., and M. Huberman
1994 *Qualitative Data Analysis*, New ed. Beverly Hills, CA: Sage.

Miller, J., and M. Kirk
1986 *Reliability and Validity in Qualitative Research*. Newbury Park, CA: Sage.

Qualitative Sociology
1991 (Special Edition on Qualitative Computing.)

Richards, L., and T.J. Richards
1991a "Computing in Qualitative Analysis: A Healthy Development? *Qualitative Health Research* 1: 234-262.

Richards, L., and T.J. Richards
1991b "The Transformation of Qualitative Method: Computational Paradigms and Research Processes." Pp. 38-53 in *Using Computers in Qualitative Analysis*, edited by N. Fielding and R. Lee. Berkeley,CA: Sage.

Richards, L., and T.J. Richards
1994 "From Filing Cabinet to Computer. In *Analysing Qualitative Data*, edited by R.W. Burgess and A. Bryman. London: Routledge.

Richards, L., and D. Simon
1993 "Making the Change: Report From a Project Designed for Qualitative Computing." Unpublished.

Richards, L., N. Davis, C. Lewis, C. Maisano, and C. Seibold
1994 "Computing the Change: Report on a Team Project Designed for Qualitative Computing." Paper to Qualitative Health Research Conference, Hershey, Pennsylvania, June.

Richards, L., C. Parsons, and V. Seeger
1994 "Women's Perceptions of Risk in Midlife: Grounded Theory and Computer-Assisted Analysis." Second International Qualitative Health Research Conference, Hershey, Pennsylvania.

Richards, L., C. Seibold, and D. Simon
1993 "Putting Everything on Hold: The Family Contexts of Women's Experiences in Midlife." Fourth Australian Family Research Conference, Sydney.

Richards, T., and L. Richards
1991c "The NUDIST System." *Qualitative Sociology* 14: 289-306.

Richards, T., and L. Richards
1994 "Using Computers in Qualitative Analysis." In *Handbook of*

Qualitative Research, edited by N. Denzin and Y. Lincoln. Newbury Park, CA: Sage.

Seibold, C., D. Simon, and L. Richards
1994 "Feminist Method and Qualitative Research about Midlife." *Advanced Journal of Nursing* 19.

Singh, S.
Forthcoming "Money and Marriage and the Computer." *Marriage and Family Review.*

Strauss, A. L.
1987 *Qualitative Analysis for Social Scientists.* New York: Cambridge University Press.

Tesch, R.
1990 *Qualitative Research: Analysis Types and Software Tools.* Basingstoke: Falmer.

Wall, E.
1995 "The Problem with NUDISTs." *Society/Societe* 19(1)(March):13-14.

Weitzman and Miles
1995 *Computer Programs for Qualitative Analysis* Thousand Oaks, CA: Sage.

FROM CODING TO HYPERTEXT:
STRATEGIES FOR MICROCOMPUTING AND QUALITATIVE DATA ANALYSIS

Anna Weaver and Paul Atkinson

INTRODUCTION

Recent years have seen something of a revolution in the storage and retrieval of data for qualitative analysis, in sociology, anthropology, education, psychology, and cognate disciplines. In the course of the past decade there has been increasing use of computer software for qualitative analysis. Numerous applications have been developed specifically for the purpose, and generic software has been used for various analytic tasks. The general approach has come to be referred to as Computer Assisted Qualitative Data Analysis (CAQDAS). The state of play is currently confused. There is considerable overlap in the functions

Studies in Qualitative Methodology, Volume 5, pages 141-168.

ISBN: 1-55938-902-8.

provided by various programs, although there are also key differences as well. No researcher or research group is likely to need all the available software, and principled choices are encouraged by all commentators. Fielding (1993) for instance notes the need for review and evaluation and suggests that the uncritical adoption and implementation of particular CAQDAS software packages—or indeed the wholesale endorsement of the approach—may commit researchers to the implicit adoption of particular research strategies.

Hitherto, however, there has been relatively little attempt at systematic comparison and review of the applications, together with a thorough and critical analysis of the fundamental methodology. Equally, there remains a need for critical reflection by analysts of their own implementation of microcomputing strategies. It is, therefore, clear that the research community needs systematic appraisal of complementary or contrasting computing strategies in the analysis of qualitative, textual data for the social sciences.

Here we report one attempt to undertake a systematic comparison of complementary and contrasting strategies for the computer-assisted analysis of qualitative data. Before embarking on our more detailed discussion, we describe the general features of the research project. Unlike the vast majority of commentaries in this area, our own work is grounded neither in one particular software application nor in an empirical research project of our own. The project was designed entirely in *methodological* terms, and was aimed entirely at critical reflection on the methodological implications of various approaches. The core of the project, therefore, consisted of a systematic review of microcomputing *strategies* rather than a comprehensive review of all the available software.

There have been various publications that outline and review CAQDAS (e.g., Agar 1983; Brent 1984; Brent et al. 1987; Gerson 1987; Heise 1988; Lee and Fielding 1991; Pfaffenberger 1988; Shelly and Sibert 1986; Tesch 1988, 1990, 1991). Likewise, there is a small but growing literature on individual researchers' own experiences and advice concerning their own use of software applications (e.g., Cordingley 1991; Walker 1993). Most notably,

Tesch (1990) offers an excellent overview of the software available when her text was completed. Much of the literature is concerned with either "advocacy" or "consumer reports." Several authors in the field have been responsible for the development of particular software products, and focus their own attention on the benefits of their chosen approach (cf. Richards and Richards 1991a, 1991b; Dey 1993). They all have the general limitation, however, that they cannot provide comparative reviews of the software when tested on identical data. It was a particular feature of our own research that we applied various computing strategies to the *same* set of data. As a consequence we were able to concentrate on the *processes* of data analysis rather than specific substantive outputs; and on the general methodological consequences of those analytic strategies rather than the detailed documentation of one or another software product.

Rather than base our project on ethnographic work of our own, therefore, we decided to use a preexisting set of qualitative data, We used field data collected by Julius Roth in the course of his research on social relations in tuberculosis sanitaria. Roth's study is well known as a classic example of a sociologist turning personal adversity to professional advantage, in that having contracted TB he kept a journal of his experiences as an in-patient. He also undertook a period of fieldwork as a full participant, employed as an "attendant" in a hospital. He also undertook fieldwork as an overt ethnographer. His research is a uniquely valuable case study, in that he published a monograph (Roth 1963) and a series of papers about his field experiences, and in addition, he has made copies of his field data available to scholars for methodological purposes. For the purposes of this particular project we used the data set derived from Roth's period of work as a hospital attendant. The data had already been edited in the interests of confidentiality: Roth had substituted pseudonyms, for example. We based our own methodological exercises on samples of the field notes written up by Roth over a period of about 100 days of work. The notes were word-processed into text files—one file per day of notes—and transformed into ASCII files, ready to be imported into any of the applications we wanted to use.

It was, therefore, a particular feature of this project that we came initially to the data "cold." In other words, we had no particular preconceptions about them, nor did we have personal investments in "findings." One of us, Atkinson, was familiar with Roth's published work; Weaver was familiar with neither the data nor the published output. It was thus possible for us to approach the storage, retrieval, and analysis of the data as a set of technical, methodological tasks. We were not preoccupied with producing a "best" analysis of the data, as we might have been had we been trying to work on data of our own. Substantive issues could safely be treated as subordinate to methodological considerations. There are, of course, problems inherent in such a strategy. By and large, field notes are not constructed with the interests of secondary analysis in mind. Even when—as in this case—authors are willing to share them with a wider intellectual community, the data themselves reflect their original composition as field notes constructed for subsequent use by their author.

It is not unknown for scholars to undertake a secondary analysis of ethnographic data of others and the problems of such work have been documented by others (e.g., Lutkehaus 1990). Here is not the place for us to comment in detail about the interpretive problems involved in such a secondary analysis, nor on the adequacy of the data qua data. We intend to do so elsewhere. Suffice it to say that the animation of a "cold" or "inert" body of field data is by no means straightforward. The methodological gains of temporal and personal distance from the data were to some extent offset by the lack of personal, *tacit* knowledge about the social setting and actors in question. Field data (any data) can never provide an exhaustive description or account of the social action and its contexts. In most ethnographic research, the analyst and the field researcher are one and the same (or members of the same team) and personal knowledge can be drawn on, In the course of this project we were forced to rely on the "data" alone, recognizing that the field notes were but a partial reflection not only of the social setting they described, but also of the research process itself. Nevertheless, the use of a "cold" data set undoubtedly encouraged us to focus attention on *how* we were to make sense of it. They also forced on us an essentially inductive approach to the data, in that we approached them without our own "hunches" or "foreshadowed problems."

In setting about the meta-analytic project we set a number of limits on the computing environment and the software we were to examine. First, we chose to operate entirely within an MS-DOS/Windows context. All our work was undertaken on PC machines. We therefore excluded software designed exclusively for the MAC environment (notably those that use the MAC Hypercard, such as HYPERQUAL or HYPERSOFT). This was not based on any qualitative judgments concerning the respective operating systems. Rather, the decision reflected our own working environment and the fact that the majority of users in the United Kingdom use PCs. It was, therefore, a pragmatic decision rather than a reflection of any profound evaluations or prejudices concerning microcomputing environments per se. Second, we made no attempt to review all available software. We concentrated rather on *strategies* of data storage, retrieval, and analysis.

In this paper we concentrate our efforts on contrasting analytic strategies, and use one main software package to illustrate each of them. They by no means exhaust all the analytic or software possibilities. We do not make these selections in order to endorse or recommend the particular software; nor indeed should any critiques or reservations be taken to imply recommendation for a competitor. Our choice is principled, however. Our first strategy is that of "coding" the data, or more fully, a "code-and-retrieve" strategy. The core, representative software package used to exemplify this approach was The Ethnograph (Seidel, Kjolseth, and Seymour 1988). It is almost certainly the most widely used and best documented among the family of applications (others include the Text Analysis Package and Textbase Alpha). Indeed, our informal contacts with other qualitative researchers suggest that The Ethnograph has certainly until recently in the United Kingdom been the "application of choice" for many individuals and groups using PCs. (Hyperqual occupies a similar position for MAC users, we suspect.) Moreover, the "coding" of data has become almost synonymous with CAQDAS in some quarters. (We used Version 3 of The Ethnograph; version 4.0 has various improvements but was not available to us when we undertook the analysis.)

The second, contrasting, strategy we used was "Hypertext." As we shall see, this can imply a quite radically different approach not only to the analysis of qualitative data, but also to its presentation. It has potentially profound implications for the *representation* of ethnographic research and of social realities. It stands at the opposite end of the spectrum of analytic approaches from The Ethnograph. We used GUIDE, a commercially available generic Hypertext program that runs under Windows. We used its basic features in developing an analytic strategy to exemplify the general approach.

In focusing attention here on just the two analytic strategies we are fully aware of the fact that we do not cover the entire spectrum of software types and their use for CAQDAS. We omit from this discussion the use of software designed for content-analysis, bulk-indexing, and the like. In our general project, we explored such a strategy using FYI3000Plus, and elsewhere we argue that, simple though they may be, such lexical searching is a useful adjunct to the "coding" strategy: it can be a particularly useful part of early exploration within the database (Weaver and Atkinson 1994). Among the more significant software applications we omit here (though not from our general meta-analysis) are those, such as KWALITAN and NUD•IST, that are designed to go beyond the somewhat elementary procedures associated with The Ethnograph. They are based on a more thoroughgoing representation of "grounded theory," and are designed to facilitate "theory building" rather than just the mechanical tasks of coding and retrieving segments of textual data. Our use of KWALITAN and NUD•IST is reported elsewhere (Weaver and Atkinson 1994).

In the remainder of the paper we shall outline and comment on our use of the two selected strategies. After comparing them both, we shall present a summary of our own experience of implementing the Hypertext strategy. We shall discuss how each computing strategy implies a distinctive view of "the data" and of "analysis" itself. The burden of our commentary is that no use of computing in CAQDAS is innocent or transparent. None is a purely mechanical or automatic emulation of an ideal "qualitative data analysis." Each approach inscribes particular presuppositions; each furnishes its own possibilities and limitations; each carries with it dangers as well as opportunities.

CODE-AND-RETRIEVE (THE ETHNOGRAPH)

We spent some time implementing The Ethnograph as an exemplar of the code-and-retrieve approach. It is reasonably representative of that family of software, and is now widely used and well understood. Its basic procedure is simple enough. It is dependent on the familiar notion of "coding." Code words are attached to segments of text (identified by line-numbers marking the start and end of each coded segment) and are then used to search the data files in order to retrieve segments identified with the same codes.

The underlying logic is essentially based on the manual procedures developed before the advent of microcomputers. The data were once physically disaggregated by literally cutting up hard copy and distributing the fragments to physical files; or, they were marked and indexed in some way within the continuous record. The analytic logic remains one of "de-contextualizing" and "re-contextualizing" segments of data (cf. Tesch 1990). That is, the fragments are detached from the other data in which they were originally embedded, and relocated in an analytic file or category.

Software such as The Ethnograph does rather more than just the copy-and-paste function, however (which could be achieved by most good word processors). The Ethnograph facilitates multiple coding of segments; codes may overlap and may be nested within one another. Segments may be retrieved using single or multiple searches. In the latter case, the program will retrieve segments according to the co-occurrence of two or more code words. In principle, therefore, The Ethnograph allows codes to be combined in an approximation of Boolean logic in order to facilitate complex search-and-retrieval procedures.

The number of codes per segment is limited in The Ethnograph, and we repeatedly found ourselves running up against those limits. In coding the Roth data we found ourselves needing to specify dense and complex coding systems. Recognizing that "thin" coding was not a satisfactory way of exploiting the full search-and-retrieve capacities of the software, we devised coding schemes of varying degrees of abstractness. We therefore differentiated between codes of different types. They included sets of codes of an abstract, generic level at one extreme, and specific, topical ones at the other. We also included "cast" codes, used to identify social actors present and actors referred to in the speech of others. A combination of thematic, topical, and cast codes were supplemented with a number of "episode codes" (attached to enable particular events or stretches of action to be retrieved easily). These could rapidly exhaust the limits of The Ethnograph for any one text segment. There are practical solutions that we devised, but limitations of this sort may implicitly encourage rather "thin" coding schemes on the part of the inexperienced analyst, tempted or directed to attach only a restricted number of codes to a given set of data.

A dense and comprehensive coding of the Roth data called for a careful design and implementation of a coding scheme. Analysts using the Ethnograph need to spend a considerable amount of time devising and experimenting with codes. Coding calls for a considerable investment in preliminary analyses, if codes are to be devised and added in a systematic way. Searching and retrieving data will only be useful if the coding scheme is adequate in the first place. The Ethnograph allows the analyst to change, delete, or add codes at any stage; in theory the processes of coding and re-coding may follow the emergence of ideas. Coding may, in theory, be "grounded" in processes of data analysis. The tasks of entering and deleting codes are laborious and tedious, however. We strongly suspect that in many projects, coding schemes will become "frozen" once the data have been worked through and coded for the first time. Rather than promoting flexible analyses and emergent ideas—as advocated under the rubric of "grounded theory"—our experience suggests that software like The Ethnograph may have the unintended consequence of promoting a somewhat *static* approach, in which both "data" and "codes" become frozen. In the course of our own project, once the data had been coded and the codes entered into The Ethnograph, there was little further insight or "discovery" about the materials. The Ethnograph software is also poor in representing relationships *between* codes. In essence, the coding strategy is a "flat" one.

Moreover the limitation of its quasi-Boolean logic (X and Y, X not Y) severely diminishes the possibility of combining codes (X or Y) as categories within a superordinate code. It is, therefore, not possible to move from specific to more general categories through the search procedures. A complete, and time-consuming, re-coding would be necessary.

The retrieval of coded data is not problematic in itself. Indeed, it is a mechanistic exercise. It is not primarily an "analytic" process in itself. We found that the creative work, and our "discoveries" about the data took place at the *coding* stage. The practicalities of coding undoubtedly resulted in a comprehensive and detailed reflection on the structure and content of the data. The need to construct an adequate coding scheme forced us to consider how best to represent our ideas, and to be alert as to possible relationships between the categories we devised. To that extent, therefore, the software facilitated the swift and comprehensive searching of the data. It also encouraged thorough exploration and coding. Its effective use necessitates careful thought about categories and codings. On the other hand, it offered no conceptual advance over manual approaches. It claims to do little toward analysis or conceptual development, as opposed to storage and retrieval.

The Ethnograph facilitates some aspects of "grounded theory" data handling. As we have indicated, it emulates manual searching more efficiently and comprehensively. But its version of coding recapitulates what Atkinson (1992) has called "the culture of fragmentation" as a general approach to qualitative analysis. That is, it reflects the implicit assumption that data reduction and aggregation lie at the heart of the task; it can readily lead to a quasi-positivist version of "analysis." The implicit model of coding it draws on is by no means identical to that advocated by proponents of "grounded theory," such as Anselm Strauss (1987); although it must also be acknowledged that Strauss himself seems to have embraced a rather more mechanistic view of coding more latterly (see Strauss and Corbin 1990; and see Glaser 1992 for a vigorous denunciation).

HYPERTEXT (GUIDE)

Hypertext—here represented by GUIDE—is a strategy that facilitates (indeed demands) flexible and varied approaches to the characterization of a textual database. The software permits the analyst to create and trace multiple links and pathways through the data. The general features of GUIDE facilitate a number of basic functions that are then used in the analytic tasks:

1. "*Note buttons.*" These use pop-up Windows, and are a useful means of adding information to the data (such as background information about the actors involved). Because the notes appear in pop-up Windows the analyst can make constant reference to the data when making or consulting notes; likewise, the notes are readily referred to while reading the data.
2. "*Reference buttons.*" These are used to create links between items of information within the data. They may, for instance, link chunks of data relating to a single topic. The paragraphs containing the relevant topic or reference may be linked together so as to create a "trail." Within such a trail the analyst can browse surrounding text; he or she can move from data in the trail to information *about* the trail (such as notes and comments). New trails can be created and old trails revisited at any point in the analysis. Equally, reference links may be created between notes or memoranda. Finally, reference buttons can be used to create links between the data and other "objects" such as charts, glossaries, contents lists, and so on.
3. "*Expansion buttons.*" Expansion buttons create vertical links. For instance, activating an expansion button in the data will unfold the researcher's analytical comments on them and, in turn, reveal buttons to analytic memoranda that relate to those data. Thus, the analytic memoranda (whatever their form and content) are always linked directly to the data themselves and can be activated very easily. Memoranda of different sorts and at different levels of generality can be created, and links between them

maintained. In our analysis of the Roth data, for instance, we distinguished between "Analytic Notes," "Topical Memoranda," and "Thematic Memoranda" (moving from local to generic levels of analysis).

GUIDE can perform tasks similar to a code-and-retrieve strategy. The researcher is able to reassemble in one place all pieces of text from various locations in the field notes otes or transcripts identified as having a common reference. This is not achieved by attaching code words, however. Rather, the analyst copies relevant segments of the data into another document (i.e., a copy-and-paste procedure). The latter may be another GUIDE file, or a word processor document (requiring minor formatting changes). Either of those are preferable to the kind of files produced by software such as The Ethnograph. Furthermore, when the data are thus reaggregated in GUIDE, the analyst can include additional commentary or contextual information, as hidden text, activated by a note button. Additionally, because both GUIDE and the word processor operate in a Windows environment, researchers may work with both applications simultaneously—copying from GUIDE documents into word processing documents. Moreover, entire documents can be imported into GUIDE documents: links can therefore be created between, say, research papers, memoranda, and data. A suitable bibliographic manager, such as PAPYRUS, running under Windows will also permit analytic and data documents to be merged with bibliographic references.

However, the analyst using GUIDE is by no means restricted to the equivalent of a code-and-retrieve approach. GUIDE provides a genuine Hypertext approach. This uses the "buttons" functions fully, and exploits the opportunity to create "links." By activating links, "trails" through the data may be manipulated and activated at any point during analysis. Consequently, it is not necessary to de-contextualize and re-contextualize data (as in The Ethnograph) at all. Analytic memoranda, or preliminary analyses, do not need to contain segments of data: data and memoranda are linked through reference buttons.

With a fully realized Hypertext application, such as GUIDE, there is no real distinction between "data" and other materials such as memoranda. This high degree of integration and consequent flexibility may facilitate an analytic approach that is more faithful to the cognitive tasks and intellectual presuppositions of "classic" ethnographic inquiry. It may also accommodate individual differences in analytic strategy between different researchers or research groups more readily than the more prestructured applications. The opportunity to create multiple links and trails may encourage the analyst to pursue dense networks of association and meaning. The goals of "thick description" may thus be promoted. (No software can guarantee such analyses, of course.)

The Hypertext strategy implemented in GUIDE allows the analyst to move from the data "upwards" toward generic concepts, and toward theory-building. It is, however, equally possible to work from "top" to "bottom." A more deductive approach to theory-testing may be taken, working from theoretical concepts downward through analytic memoranda to the data. This opportunity to follow "trails" in any direction would be especially valuable in the conduct of a secondary analysis: decisions and their analytic consequences may be explored by subsequent analysts.

GUIDE is not without its problems and limitations. First, it has a problem common to Hypertext applications: it may be dangerously easy for the analyst to become "lost in hyperspace." It is indeed possible to lose one's place within the multiplicity of links, levels, Windows, trails, and so on. A further, and profound, issue relates to the actual process of analysis and the representation of its results in texts. The implications are far-reaching. The trails facilitated by GUIDE do not lend themselves to the production of simple texts. Except where emulating a code-and-retrieve approach, GUIDE does not facilitate the printing out of a "linear" textual product. On the other hand, Hypertext may ultimately prove to be not simply a tool for the production of conventional analyses and ethnographic texts; rather, it may prove a mode of presentation in its own right. We shall comment on these issues in a more speculative vein in the concluding section of this paper.

ANALYTICAL WORK WITH HYPERTEXT

As we have suggested, there is current need for two complementary approaches to CAQDAS. On the one hand, there needs to be research that is specifically methodological, explicitly concerned with evaluating software. Hitherto our paper has been in that first vein. On the other hand, there is a need for reflective autobiographical accounts about particular experiences of working with software. In this section we turn to the latter. We reflect on our first experience of using GUIDE, and discuss some of the ways in which Hypertext transforms analytic techniques. As we do so we shall continue to make comparison with The Ethnograph, in order to illustrate contrasting strategies of "knowing" the data.

As we have seen, Hypertext involves the construction of documents, buttons, links, and trails; and movement between and revision of those structures in pursuit of an analytic question. What is particularly distinctive about Hypertext is that both those activities continue throughout analysis. Indeed, they cannot be distinguished from each other because, in practice, they merge into and shape each other. To illustrate these aspects of Hypertext, wc shall now outline some of the activities and decisions undertaken in our own research project, when using GUIDE for the very first time.

To set the scene: the GUIDE manual had been read, and the tutorial supplied with the software had been worked through, so we had some idea of the potential of GUIDE, and how to manipulate its most important functions. Second, the data had been entered into GUIDE from ASCII files, by using its "place text" function. This had been a straightforward process. A directory called "ROTHDATA" had been set up, into which all the data were placed. Since the data were field notes, and data files consisted of days of data, distinctions between files were more a matter of convenience than analytical significance. So it seemed that rigid separation into files imposed artificial boundaries between them. We sought to overcome this by linking each data file to the next, in chronological order, with the last linking back to the first, thus forming a loop or something analogous to a "hypercard stack." This was achieved by making reference buttons for "next day" and "last day" at the top of each file. This would enable the data to be treated as a whole later, and also enabled easy navigation between files. Apart from its practical implications, this rather mechanical task also provided the ideal opportunity for us to practice creating buttons and links.

It seemed that the clearest way of exploring the possibilities with GUIDE, and learning how to optimize them, was to explore a particular question. We therefore pursued an analytic theme that we had identified from our previous work with these data. It is one of central importance in the understanding of any such clinical setting where infectious diseases are treated: "how do the various actors define the role of bugs and germs in the infection of persons and space with TB, and what social factors shape these ideas?" In order to tackle our question, we began by entering the bottom layer of the Hypertext—the data—and opened the first day of field notes. With our question in mind, we started browsing the document, getting an idea of the vocabulary, jotting down on paper words of interest, such as bugs, germs, dirt, disease, so that a lexical search on them could be conducted later.

After several data documents had been browsed for this purpose, and the list of keywords seemed to have been fairly exhaustive, a new document was created: this was to be our first analytic memo. On its first lines the analytical question was typed, and then a space was allocated for each keyword on our list. Each occurrence of the keywords, and their surrounding lexical context, was to be pasted into the relevant place in this document. We then returned to the first and, using the find function, searched for every occurrence of our keywords in the data as a whole. (This is possible without having to open each document individually, because of the search option "active and linked." This is an important reason for linking all data documents together at the outset.)

As each occurrence of the keyword was found, its lexical context was read, and a decision was made about where the boundaries of the segment were to be (although it was realized that it did not matter too much since the context of the segment could be easily retrieved, as noted shortly). The segment was copied into the clipboard and then pasted into the relevant space of the new document. Segments in the new document could then be made into expansion buttons, and analytical notes elaborating on the meaning of the segment in terms of the particular question concerning the document could be written in expansions. This is the first major difference between re-contextualized documents in GUIDE and The Ethnograph, since the latter provides no facility of writing notes into to the documents themselves.

Establishing those re-contextualized documents was quite a lengthy process. This is because we believed that, in order to optimize some of the most unique and beneficial aspects of Hypertext, it would be necessary to link each of the segments in the new document to their original location in the field notes. This is the second way in which the re-contextualization of data with GUIDE may be differentiated from that of traditional coding approaches. (Indeed it was recognized that even this duplication of segments was not really necessary. It would probably be more efficient to link a reference button in the new document called something like "eg 1" to the source instead, but the researchers, not used to such a heavy reliance on Hypertext links, felt more comfortable with this method which seemed to make the data more readily accessible or tangible.) This belief meant that every instance of a keyword retrieved with "find" was then made into a reference button and linked to the segment in the new document. The same was established vice versa so that researchers could move in either direction during analysis: memo to data, or data to memo.

So what did this achieve? We believe that it facilitated an appreciation of a segment's holistic significance, in all its complexity, rather than perceiving it only in terms of just one predefined dimension at a time. In other words, this counterbalances the "culture of fragmentation" which characterizes so much qualitative analysis. Rather, researchers are encouraged to see the segment as *more* than merely a fragment of the data relating to a particular topic which, in turn, is but a fragment of the total analysis.

This threw up a methodological problem, however. It has long been recognized that a single segment of data is likely to be significant to many different aspects of the total analysis, or "slices" of the data. Thus, it seemed that the whole point of creating those new documents containing pasted segments as defined by their lexical content, was that a single paragraph, for example, which was relevant to many different topics and themes, could be pasted over and over again into the various memos dedicated to these topics. Each document focused the researchers' attention on analyzing the segment regarding its meaning in terms of only that topic in particular. But using our method of linking memos to data, this became problematic: it became impossible to link the actual keyword to all the pasted segments in these different documents because we would have no control in specifying which link was to be activated. Our experience with GUIDE suggested that in this situation, only the last link created is ever retrieved. Thus, we clearly needed to rethink our method of linking materials.

We then came up with the idea of placing reference buttons going to various pasted documents in expansions rather than making the keyword itself a reference button (Figure 1). The segment of interest is made into an expansion button (which is handy anyway because it highlights the segment by making it bold on screen). When activated, it reveals not only analytical notes about the segment in its original context, but also the names of pasted documents in which the segment has been recontextualized, each of which consists of a separate reference button.

This plan also had several added advantages. First, it made explicit the destination of each link because the title of the target document was the name of the button. Second, it produced a kind of data display that showed to what analytic categories the segment was related, pointing to possible relations between those categories. Finally, this plan also seemed to provide us with another means of being systematic about the distinction between different layers of analysis in the structure of the Hypertext. The bottom most layer (with all expansions closed) was reserved for data only. Any references to nondata—material in other layers of the Hypertext—could be viewed only by opening expansions. Thus we were still able to preserve what we believed to be of value earlier—the data segment may be seen in its relation to the data as a whole and independently of any classifications made by the researcher. It seemed that this method provided us with the "best of both worlds."

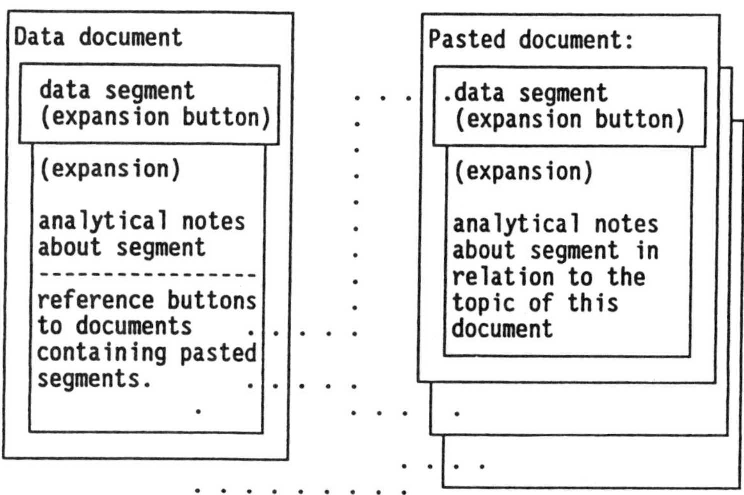

Figure 1. Reference buttons to documents containing pasted segments relating to a particular theme are located in expansions in data documents. Thus, the segment in its topical context is directly linked to the segment in its original context, and vice versa.

This also produced another idea. If the bottom layer of the Hypertext was to be for data only, reference buttons on this level should be used only for linking together types of data, such as field notes and the diaries of participants, or field notes and pictures; or else, linking together different items within or between data documents, such as words. We tested this idea by linking together every instance of the word *bug* in the Roth data documents, via the "find" facility, and making each word into a reference button to the next. The words were linked together in a way that formed a loop. This "bug trail" could be revisited at any point in the analysis. (The term *bug* was chosen as it was a recurrent folk term reported in Roth's data, used by various social actors to describe infectious agents.)

The advantage of having this trail in addition to the document containing pasted segments, is that it is independent of any interpretation of the analyst. An item's inclusion is decided solely by its lexical content rather than a decision regarding its relation to any analytical question or theme. It was anticipated that similar lexical trails would be set up for other words of interest. This type of trail proved to be particularly valuable for tasks which sought to establish the meanings that a certain term holds for persons in the field. At a more general and theoretical level, lexical trails may contribute useful insights to how common meanings are shaped and reproduced in a given social setting.

Of course, lexical searching of a general sort may be achieved by many software applications, including those produced for content analysis and bulk-indexing. The particular value of programs like GUIDE in this respect is the fact that Hypertext consists of many different parts (for example: data, working papers, various types of memos), each having their own particular structure and function, and the lexical trail is but one part. Furthermore, not only does GUIDE contain all these different parts, but it also supports a high degree of interaction between them via soft buttons. The implication is that GUIDE does not force its user to conduct lexical searches, construct trails, and focus on language. On the other hand, it may introduce a lexical approach to an analysis which would have otherwise been confined to a coding strategy. Finally, the high degree of interaction between the various components of the Hypertext enables the creation and revisiting of a lexical trail to be combined with other activities such as reading or writing an analytic memo about the trail, or a glossary in which all the uses of a given word are listed. Indeed, such documents may be defined as part of the trail.

From this description of a session of analysis with GUIDE which aimed, more than anything else, to develop a means of systematically organizing the structure of the Hypertext, a picture emerges of the kinds of patterns of work that are intrinsic to Hypertext for these decisions were largely about the organization of information. They were also responses to questions such as "in what situations do we want, or not want, certain information to be displayed?" and "How can we best ensure that information is not lost, or indeed that *we* do not become lost, in 'hyperspace'?"

These sorts of questions are, of course, never raised in relation to work with non-Hypertext programs.

Such organizational problems are particularly salient in the early stages of using GUIDE for analysis. This means that they are complicated by the fact that researchers are faced with trying to organize, or make room for, something that has not yet developed. However, it is anticipated that when GUIDE has been used once, such questions become less troublesome, because researchers will be accustomed to shaping GUIDE to fit their analytic style. Since GUIDE has so little predefined structure, researchers need to carve some structure into it to make it do qualitative analysis effectively. Indeed, this goes for not only the way they use GUIDE to organize information, but also the way they get GUIDE to behave. By using the high level programming language (LOGiiX) embedded in GUIDE, researchers can author GUIDE to create a shell which is specifically designed for their particular style of qualitative analysis, and into which any research project can be fed. (Anna Weaver is presently working on authoring GUIDE specifically for qualitative analysis to see how feasible this possibility is.)

A more enduring organizational problem, however, is ensuring that all objects, and their location, are systematically recorded. Our method of doing this was to enter the name of each new object into a specialized document, which was divided into themes and topics, and which acted like a contents page. Each item was then made into a reference button, enabling the direct retrieval of the desired object. The page was programmed to appear whenever GUIDE was loaded, and remain in the background of the screen at all times so it was always at hand. However, many objects may be created within one session when using GUIDE, and remembering to update the contents page is not easy, at least until this activity becomes habitual. It is also time-consuming. Furthermore, even the way items are organized on the contents page at some point becomes problematic: its relevance to a theme may change over time, requiring the button to be moved.

It needs to be emphasized that, because there is so much freedom in organizing both data and analytical material—or indeed the research as a whole—with GUIDE, not all researchers would have used it in the way described here. This is because what seems desirable or "natural" to researchers depends largely on their prior experiences. Indeed, this raises questions regarding our way of utilizing GUIDE. For example, would we have engaged in the activity of copying and pasting if we had not previously used the Ethnograph, which relies wholly on this activity? And would we have created a lexical trail if we had not used a similar strategy before? These questions are difficult to answer, but it certainly seems that our preference to copy segments into analytical memoranda, rather than relying on jumping between documents, would be due to a dependence on duplication—the central principle of the coding strategy. Thus, exposure to other methods to some extent shapes the way Hypertext is used.

The way Hypertext is used also seems to depend on the degree to which the data have been exposed to the researchers, and the degree to which a relationship has developed between the two. Although this research consisted of a secondary analysis, the data had already been examined using other strategies before utilizing GUIDE, so we had already established a close acquaintance with the data. Thus, the activities we have described are probably more akin to the average ethnographic project than normal secondary analysis, or research where the tasks of data collection and data analysis are allocated to different people, where analysts approach the data "cold." Thus, in such cases, how may GUIDE support ways of penetrating the data at the very outset of analysis, if researchers have very little knowledge of the data? Hypertext does this in several ways.

Unlike the Ethnograph, GUIDE does not assume a degree of familiarity with data before it is utilized. The Ethnograph forces the researcher to become familiar with the data by requiring a hard copy of the data to be coded manually before the program can be used. Indeed, even before the activity of manual coding can begin, some idea of an organizing system needs to have been developed. Thus it seems that reading the hard copy of data, and jotting down marginal comments, is the fundamental analytic activity when using The Ethnograph, and the one which familiarizes researchers with their data in the first instance. This means, of course, that familiarity with data is bounded within constraints of chronology, or the linear order of the field notes, or the ordering of interviews.

In order to use GUIDE, however, there are no rigid divisions between data preparation and analysis. Indeed, secondary researchers may glance at data for the first time after they have been placed into GUIDE, which is impossible with The Ethnograph. Analysis with GUIDE involves developing an organizing system while online and using it to activate data. It intervenes much earlier in the analysis than does The Ethnograph.

Guide supports browsing more than any other strategy. Indeed, browsing has an active, causal role, being the means by which the data are shaped early on in analysis. In the very first session of analysis, while browsing, researchers can highlight interesting segments, add first thoughts about such segments in expansions in data files, and link together related paragraphs or related documents, or items in documents. Furthermore, this activity ignites ideas about themes in the data, and even embryonic hypotheses which researchers may want to store somewhere separately, jotting down future aims. Here, they may create a new document which is concerned specifically with recording new analytical paths to be examined and analytical problems, rather than substantive theories or the actual content of analysis. The conceptual structure of our Hypertext is illustrated in Figure 2. Of course, the actual structure is much more complex than this, with established individual trails weaving within and between these layers.

From this discussion it is clear that Hypertexts offers new and exciting possibilities for many qualitative researchers. The fact that they are new, of course, means that old methods have been transformed, and may be even lost in a Hypertext approach. They also come at a cost: Hypertext implies new organizational dilemmas, some of which remain of concern up until the very end of analysis. But such are the costs of a flexible approach to data analysis, where inevitable shifts in ideas may be easily accommodated and indeed encouraged. At any rate, the decision about whether to use GUIDE (or indeed any software for qualitative analysis) needs to be a careful one, to ensure that its particular representation of knowledge is suitable for the aims of

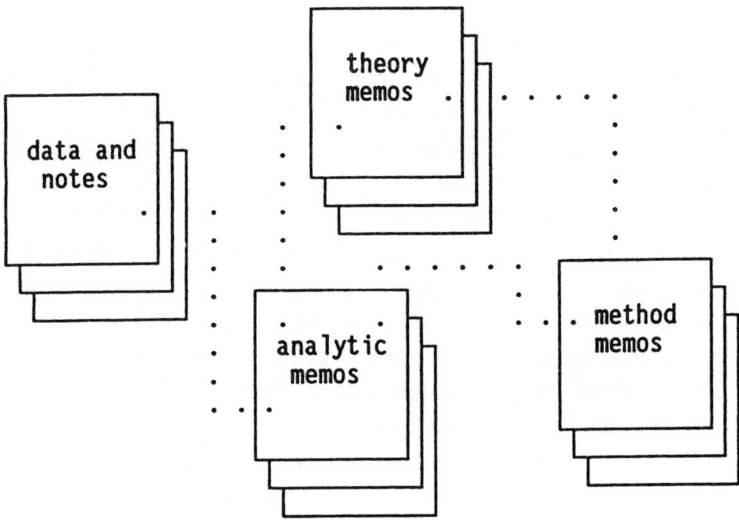

Figure 2. Conceptual Structure of the Hypertext Organized for Qualitative Analysis

the research at hand. There is also a need for researchers to be reflective about their use of a particular program throughout analysis, and make this explicit to others.

CONCLUSION

Our work has been informed by a basic assumption: that the choice of computational strategy is not just a technical matter. While CAQDAS cannot conceivably substitute for the analyst's sociological or anthropological imagination, and cannot totally determine the processes and outcomes of analysis, it should not be seen as a purely transparent, mechanistic matter either. This, of course, applies to any method of data handling and transformation. The computational possibilities of, say, factor analysis, or clustering, or multidimensional scaling have led directly to preferred modes of explanation in psychology, education, sociology, and other social disciplines, for example. Equally, the opportunities and outputs facilitated by CAQDAS may imply particular versions of analysis and interpretation. The adoption of one or another strategy may tacitly commit the analyst to a view of "data" and their treatment, foreclosing on other possibilities, while implicitly endorsing a model of research that is inscribed in the software.

It is for that reason that we have based our discussion on the juxtaposition of two opposed computing strategies for their very evident differences help to point up their contrasting methodological implications. It is our contention that the "coding" and "Hypertext" strategies can embody quite different presuppositions about data, their analysis, and their representation. Moreover, the one is a genuinely innovative possibility; the other is more of a recapitulation of data-retrieval and analysis strategies predating the full possibilities of microcomputing.

As we have suggested, the code-and-retrieve approach embodied in The Ethnograph recapitulates the kind of "cutting up" and "filing" procedures that were widely advocated in methods textbooks and courses long before the advent of CAQDAS. None the worse for that in itself, of course, The Ethnograph incorporates an analytic strategy that emphasizes the disaggregation of the original data into discrete chunks. Notwithstanding the sophistication that the codes can overlap and be embedded (a valuable addition), the very rationale of the procedure is predicated on the *segmentation* of textual data (such as field notes or transcripts). As we have indicated above, the coding of segments clearly reflects a well-entrenched approach to data handling: what we have called "the culture of fragmentation" (Atkinson 1992). This approach in turn aligns such qualitative data handling with familiar, conventional—even "positivist"—modes of analysis. It is, as we have seen, predicated on the disaggregation and reaggregation of data. Its realization via microcomputing undoubtedly permits the analyst to undertake such search-and-retrieve procedures quickly and thoroughly. The Ethnograph and software like it encourage the analyst to undertake comprehensive searches of the data set. They clearly may help to guard against the hasty, impressionistic identification of data fragments (the first that comes to hand, the most striking example ...). Likewise, the analyst is likely to have to confront the presence of negative or marginal cases (if any), and the distribution of cases within the data. Nonetheless there is little or nothing in the functions of The Ethnograph itself that *transforms* qualitative analysis. On the contrary, it seems to embody a somewhat conservative version of data handling and analysis. It is a good deal *less* than a thoroughly innovative approach to qualitative, interpretative research. Its ultimate contribution to methodological development is bound to be limited by its underlying logic.

By contrast, the approaches facilitated by Hypertext strategies seem to offer a genuinely innovative style of data handling and presentation that fully exploits the current capacities of microcomputing software. (We recognize that changes in hardware and software will continue to drive further innovations in this field.) The possibilities offered by Hypertext applications, such as GUIDE, HYPERCARD, and their relatives, suggest analytic strategies that are uniquely dependent on the capacities of contemporary microcomputing strategies. Moreover, the innovative possibilities seem—potentially—in line with current epistemological approaches to ethnographic representation. There is a clear danger of "hyping" Hypertext, and of over-selling its potential. We have no intention of becoming over-enthusiastic advocates of this strategy. We have indicated above that Hypertext is not without its problems. Equally, we do not wish to endorse novelty in this area just for the sake of it. On the other hand, the technology here seems to open up possibilities that deserve lively exploration and rigorous evaluation.

One of the most interesting and revolutionary aspects of Hypertext is the way it encourages rapid and easy switches between different analytical activities. It supports different ways of approaching and representing the data. Physically, what emerges is a complex network of intersecting trails. Cognitively, that demands a high degree of decision making when maneuvering around this network. We argue, however, that such a heavy "cognitive load" is part and parcel of a flexible and dialectical approach to data management.

Another of the most important features of Hypertext applications results in the blurring of the boundaries between "data" and "analysis" on the one hand, and between both of those and "representation" on the other. There is no need in a fully developed Hypertext environment, for instance, to force the "analysis" into the straitjacket of a single, monologic, and linear textual format. The analyst/author no longer needs to assume that his or her work will result ultimately in "an ethnography" as conventionally thought of: that is, as a "monograph" or its equivalent. The use of Hypertext software to "author" materials as well as to undertake analytic tasks, means that a highly flexible set of relationships can be facilitated: between the ethnographer and the data (and other materials) on the one hand, and between the "reader" and the ethnography on the other. These possibilities imply a different set of assumptions about what counts as reading and writing in the ethnographic research.

Here, then, is an unanticipated convergence between information technology and epistemology. In recent years commentators on ethnography (most notably from within cultural anthropology) have paid increasingly critical attention to how social realities are conventionally represented in ethnographic writing and reading. They have drawn attention not merely to the conventional and rhetorical character of ethnographic texts, but also to the ideological implications of ethnographic textual practices. A number of such commentators have aligned their criticisms with the epistemological thrust of postmodernist perspectives, arguing for ethnographic texts that are more "fragmented," more "messy," more "dialogic"; that draw on diverse literary and representational styles; that require a more active engagement on the part of their readers.

There is a direct homology between a postmodernist aesthetic and the possibilities of Hypertext. Landow (1992) has recently drawn attention to just this "convergence" between technology and epistemology. Landow has focused on the possibilities of hypermedia in the humanities. The thrust of contemporary critical theory disrupts taken-for-granted assumptions about texts, authors, and readers. It subverts the authority of the author, and the conventional surface of the text itself. It proposes a more "open" and more problematic character for textual practice. In much the same way, the possibilities of Hypertext seem to open up modes of analysis and representation that no longer privilege one single perspective and one single authorial interpretation. The "reader" can reassemble information of diverse sorts in a multiplicity of ways. Hence the work of interpretation, of *verstehen*, or reality reconstruction, is shared between the ethnographer and his or her readers, The tasks of analysis are dispersed throughout the "data" rather than being imposed upon them in a determinate manner.

ACKNOWLEDGMENTS

This paper is based on the project "Microcomputing for Qualitative Data Analysis," which was supported by ESRC research grant No. R-000-23-3200. We gratefully acknowledge the support of the ESRC. The views reported here are our own and do not represent Research Council policy. We are grateful to Julius Roth who first made his field data available to Paul Atkinson many years ago. We are grateful to Bob Burgess for his editorial help and advice, and to Martin Read for his continuing commitment to sociological computing in Cardiff. We are grateful to Amanda Coffey for her comments on a draft of this paper.

END NOTE

Version 4.0 of The Enthnograph now incorporates some features referred to as absent in version 3.0. Our general views on analytic strategies remain unchanged, however.

REFERENCES

Agar, M.
1983 "Microcomputers as Field Tools." *Computers in the Humanities*. 17: 19-26.

Atkinson, P.
1992 "Reading, Writing and Rhetoric: The Ethnography of a Medical Setting." *Qualitative Health Research* 2: 451-474.

Bolter, J.D.
1991 *Writing Space: The Computer, Hypertext, and the History of Writing*. Hillsdale, NJ: Lawrence Earlbaum.

Brent, E.
1984 "Qualitative Computing: Approaches and Issues." *Qualitative Sociology* 7: 34-60.

Brent, E., J. Scott, and J. Spencer
1987 "The Use of Computers by Qualitative Researchers." *Qualitative Sociology* 10: 309-313.

Cordingley, E.S.
1991 "The Upside and Downside of Hypertext Tools: The KANT Example." In *Using Computers in Qualitative Research*, edited by N.G. Fielding and R. Lee. London: Sage.

Dey, I.
1993 *Qualitative Data Analysis*. London: Routledge.

Fielding, N.
1993 "Analysing Qualitative Data by Computer." *Social Research Update* 1, Department of Sociology, University of Surrey.

Gerson, E.
1987 "Another Way of Working with Text." *Qualitative Sociology* 10: 204-207.

Glaser, B.
1992 *Basics of Grounded Theory Analysis*. Mill Valley, CA: Sociology Press.

Hammersley, M., and P. Atkinson
1983 *Ethnography: Principles in Practice*. London: Tavistock.

Heise, D.R.
1988 "Computer Analysis of Cultural Structures." *Social Science Computer Review* 6: 183-197.

Landow, G.P.
1992 *Hypertext: The Convergence of Contemporary Critical Theory and Technology*. Baltimore, MD: Johns Hopkins University Press.

Lee, R., and N. Fielding. (Eds).
1991 *Using Computers in Qualitative Research*. London: Sage.

Lutkehaus, N.
1990 "Refractions of Reality: On the Use of Other Ethnographers' Fieldnotes." In *Fieldnotes: The Makings of Anthropology*, edited by R. Sanjek. Ithaca, NY: Cornell University Press.

Pfaffenerber, B.
1988 *Microcomputer Applications in Qualitative Research*. Newbury Park, CA: Sage.

Richards, L., and T. Richards
1991a "Computing in Qualitative Analysis: A Healthy Development?" *Qualitative Health Research* 1: 234-262.

Richards, L., and T. Richards
1991b "The Transformation of Qualitative Method: Computational Paradigms and Research Processes." In *Using Computers in Qualitative Research*, edited by N.G. Fielding and R. Lee. London: Sage.

Roth, J.
1963 *Timetables*. Indianapolis: Bobbs-Merrill.

Seidel, J.V., R. Kjolseth, and E. Seymour
1988 *The ETHNOGRAPH: A User's Guide*. Littleton, CO: Qualis Research Associates.

Shelly, A., and E. Sibert
1986 "Using Logic-programming to Facilitate Qualitative Data Analysis." *Qualitative Sociology* 9: 145-161.

Strauss, A.L.
1987 *Qualitative Analysis for Social Scientists*. Cambridge: Cambridge University Press.

Strauss, A.L., and J. Corbin
1990 *Basics of Qualitative Research*. Newbury Park: Sage.

Tesch, R.
1988 "Computer Software and Qualitative Analysis: A Reassessment." In *New Technology in Sociology: Practical Applications in Research and Work*, edited by G. Blank, J.L. McCartney, and E. Brent. New Brunswick, NJ: Transaction Books.

Tesch, R.
1990 *Qualitative Research: Analysis Types and Software Tools*. London: Falmer.

Tesch, R.
1991 "Software for Qualitative Researchers: Analysis Needs and Program Capabilities." In *Using Computers in Qualitative Research*, edited by N.G. Fielding and R. Lee. London: Sage.

Walker, B.L.
1993 "Computer Analysis of Qualitative Data: A Comparison of Three Packages." *Qualitative Health Research* 3: 91-111.

Weaver, A., and P. Atkinson
1994 *Microcomputing and Qualitative Data Analysis*. Aldershot, Hants: Avebury.

DOING THE BUSINESS?

EVALUATING SOFTWARE PACKAGES TO AID THE ANALYSIS OF QUALITATIVE DATA SETS

Liz Stanley and Bogusia Temple

INTRODUCTION

This paper is concerned with the evaluation of a number of software packages designed to aid the analysis of qualitative data sets. The particular packages discussed are askSam, Info Select, the Ethnograph, NUD•IST, and Ethno.[1] We shall also compare these with the analytic facilities of Word for Windows.

This evaluation, in the form of a project called "Using Computers for Analysing Qualitative Data" (UCAQD), was funded by the University of Manchester as development research to underpin future research bids in the area of qualitative social science research.[2] Most university social science departments and

Studies in Qualitative Methodology, Volume 5, pages 169-193.

ISBN: 1-55938-902-8.

faculties have a good deal of expertise in using computers to aid the analysis of *quantitative* data of various kinds and in using a wide variety of suitable software in order to do so. However, it is only rarely that a comparable expertise in the area of *qualitative* data analysis exists, whether using computer software or not. This has left the onus very much on individual researchers in effect to train themselves. And while recent ESRC initiatives regarding research and graduate schools have certainly helped collectivize and professionalize the teaching of qualitative approaches more generally, there has been little integration of the use of computers and qualitative software packages in relation to such teaching.

The UCAQD project not only evaluated software but also ran a number of workshops and other related sessions on issues involved in carrying out qualitative data analysis using these packages. One result has been a very large number of local, regional, and national inquiries regarding training sessions, trials of software, and the availability of contract researchers competent in the use of such packages. Consequently another result experienced we know by others working in this area has been a good deal of pressure on us to provide such services to interested members of the research community.

Unlike many software reviews, the UCAQD project adopted the approach of evaluating such software packages "full." In our experience these packages respond very differently when used with data entered into them, compared with when "run" without data simply to look at the tools that each provides. Also they respond differently when used to aid the analysis of different kinds of qualitative data, for the data from different qualitative projects can have very different characteristics and highly varied structures.

In the UCAQD project, these five packages were used to aid the analysis of two very different data sets which had *different characteristics* in the sense of the overall size of each data set and whether different kinds of qualitative materials were involved (e.g., interviews, transcripts of meetings, ethnographic field notes), and *different structures* in the sense of the numbers of cases (i.e., the units of analysis to which segments of data are attached, and which can be persons, types of group, or a whole project) involved and the relationship between them. Word for Windows was also used to carry out a comparison of a good word processing package with the dedicated packages.

The first data set resulted from research concerned with a Women's Co-Operative Guild in a Northern ex-mill town.[3] The data set here is composed by a group of transcribed individual interviews with Co-Operative Guildswomen about their work histories within the formal and casualized sectors of the local labor market as well as within the home.

There is also a related set of transcriptions of a number of meetings of this Guild, where the same topic was the subject of group discussion.[4] In terms of the analysis that was carried out, the various components of this first data set were conceptualized as highly linked with each other, particularly around changing notions of work, the gendering of labor markets, household and labor market interconnections, and the Co-Operative Guildwomen's own perceptions and analyses of the class and gender issues involved. Indeed in some respects it was possible to see these different elements of the research—the interviews, the discussions at group meetings, and so forth—as constitutive of a highly integrated data set, with a single analysis of gender and class appropriately carried out across them, rather than, for example, keeping each element separate and focusing on differences between them. Therefore, each of these elements of the research can be seen as fitting together and as being analyzable as an integral whole.

The second data set results from research connected to an ongoing project concerned with "Mass-Observation," a popular radical social science organization active between 1937 and 1949.[5] The resultant data set here is composed by a group of day-diaries written by men and by women for Mass-Observation in response to a "directive" or set of interlinked questions, written in the Mass-Observation house-style and sent to members of Mass-Observation's National Panel in March 1990.[6]

These day-diaries can be very differently structured from each other, in the sense that their writers can utilize different notions of what "a day" is (actions carried out in hour units, descriptions of events, "inner" reflections, and so on), as well as providing what can be highly diverse content to the components of the written accounts of the panelists' days.

In terms of the analysis carried out on this second data set, the day-diaries were conceptualized as being linked primarily by virtue of being sent to Mass-Observation. What the analysis focused upon were differences in terms of how "a day" was conceptualized and inscribed by the panelists, for neither the *structure* nor the *content* of how "a day" was written about by one respondent has any necessary point of connection with any others of the respondents to this directive. It was these differences, then, that the analysis was concerned with, rather than, as in the Co-Operative Guild project, the research subjects' collective understanding of a topic. Consequently each case in the Mass-Observation project needed to be kept separate from the others, so that a "compare and contrast" analysis could be carried out. Thus, it may in a sense constitute "a whole," a single project, but it is certainly not a highly integrated one.

USING THE PACKAGES: SOME PRELIMINARIES

It is with these characteristics of our two data sets in mind that we say something about how each package is presented to potential users by its developers, what each is described as being "for" in analytic terms, and contrast this with our experience of using them in analyzing these two data sets.

The two packages which social scientists are most likely to have heard about are The Ethnograph and NUD•IST.[7] The Ethnograph, which was first distributed in the early 1980s, is described as a mechanical aid to the qualitative analyst in carrying out routine tasks such as "cut and paste" and line numbering. It rejects an approach which sees qualitative analysis as "discovering" things already "in" the data, and instead proposes, indeed insists, that qualitative analysis should actually be the articulation of the researcher's own conceptual and analytical structure. In contrast, NUD•IST, which was first distributed for the main-frame in the late 1980s before being later produced for the Macintosh and the IBM PC, adopts one version of "grounded theory." It sees itself as enabling the development of theory through identifying conceptual elements already in the data and supplied by research subjects: the researcher here pieces together what the grounded theory of subjects is.

The program askSam was first commercially distributed in the early 1980s and has been used mainly by professionals outside of the social sciences; it was in fact importantly used in analyzing the legal materials that arose from the impeachment of Richard Nixon. In effect askSam is a kind of database, although one with highly sophisticated features for handling textual data; these include unlimited field sizes and remarkable speed in linking and searching across very large numbers of both cases and flies. The program askSam shares some features with Info Select, which was developed primarily for business use and first distributed in the early 1990s. Info Select is a free text retrieval package which is promoted as organizing data and data searches in a similar way to the workings of the human mind. Here its "neuron search" is perhaps its main attraction for social scientists, because this is presented as a means of using keywords and phrases to find concepts within the data in ways seen as analogous to human thought processes.

Ethno, first distributed in the late 1980s, is different in kind rather than degree from these other packages. First, its analytic concern is with the *structure* of data and not with content; and second, it is concerned specifically with the *researcher's* conceptual structure, that is, with their interpretation of the logical connections discerned within the original data. It does not work with the original data and there is no inbuilt means for either entering this data into Ethno or of linking it to Ethno in any way. Instead what it provides is a framework for specifying and analyzing the researcher's interpretations and then presenting these in a logical diagrammatic structure.

Apart from in the case of Ethno, where it is likely to be quicker simply to re-type the product of the analysis, the results of analysis will be exported from each of these packages into a word processing package for writing up. In addition, for The Ethnograph and NUD•IST data *must* be prepared and formatted using a word processing package in particular ways before being entered, in text (or ASCII) format, into them, for they do not contain any text editing facilities. And while both askSam and Info

Select do have text editors, these are limited in their capabilities (and askSam especially so) when compared with a word processing package. Thus it makes most sense always to think of using any such package in combination with a word processing package. Moreover, some of these latter are very sophisticated pieces of software and can contain many of the features associated with qualitative analysis packages: carrying out searches using words and phrases, including with wild cards, indexing text, and writing macros, for example. Indeed, and as we shall discuss below, we have found that Word for Windows in particular provides a sufficiency of such features for an analysis of textual data to be carried out using it rather than dedicated software.

In general these software packages are presented as if there is only one way within them to analyze the data, and yet we have found that the most appropriate way to use them is in fact dependent on the characteristics of the particular data set being analyzed. Some examples may help to explain this point.

1. Both the manual and tutorial for NUD•IST encourage the user to set up the research using a hierarchical notion of the relationship between concepts. That is, the user is encouraged to "flag" particular passages which are then seen as "indexed" and to which names of the concepts these passages are seen to illustrate are then assigned, and the next step in the analytic process involves relating these concepts in a hierarchical variable tree. It is certainly possible to carry out an analysis without doing so, and indeed the manual does note how to achieve this. However, the epistemological significance and analytic consequences of working in the way encouraged by the manual and tutorial, constructing such a variable tree, are nowhere discussed. Moreover, it is possible even for experienced researchers to be led by the software rather than by their awareness of epistemological issues and debates in the discipline, and which they would be alerted to the existence of if using more conventional means of analyzing data (that is, not using dedicated software packages). A related issue concerns the way that the manual and tutorial also encourage a project's data to

be entered as a related whole. Although its separate components can in fact still be analyzed as separate cases within NUDIST (by treating them as separate "nodes" within a subsection of a variable tree), nonetheless the impetus of the package is against this, for why this procedure is significant is not explained in the manual, and so the user is most likely to pursue a project-based approach.

2. A second example is provided by various of the features of askSam. This package is extraordinarily quick at searching through very large data sets, and indeed searching through large numbers of files which are linked on a search menu (and thus the different components of a project can be easily kept within separate files). However, askSam has no inbuilt means of either line-numbering data within a particular file or of easily identifying from which of the files searched particular data segments derive. The result is that, following a search, the user is then confronted by large numbers of chunks of text with no means of identifying where these come from within the data set. Thus, in relation to both of our research projects, searches yielded amazingly quick results, but the printouts of these were hardly usable given that neither the file name nor the point in the file from which extracts come were provided by the package. Similar problems arise in using Info Select, although otherwise there are important differences between it and askSam. Info Select has no inbuilt means of line-numbering data within the "windows" that compose a "stack" of data; and it too has no means of informing the user carrying out a search from where in a "stack" any retrieved data derives, for it only specifies how many windows have been retrieved.
3. Our next example concerns the conceptual structure developed through using The Ethnograph. There are two separate but related and mutually reinforcing analytic problems here. The first is that searches within The Ethnograph are based exclusively on time-consuming detailed precoding of the data set, and analysis is not possible outside of this coding frame. The second is that if the user later decides that another frame of analysis is

preferable, then the entire process of coding has to be gone through again because it is not possible to reorganize the structure of data segments/variables from within, apart from making relatively minor changes to this structure. Thus in analyzing the Mass-Observation day-diaries, we decided to shift from an earlier emphasis on their structure to one which integrated elements of this within a focus on aspects of content. However, such a marked change in the conceptual approach proved impossible to manage through reorganization and expansion of the existing coding frame and instead we had to re-code and reconstruct the entire conceptual structure.

4. Our last example here involves Ethno. As we have already remarked, this package works exclusively as a means of analyzing the structure of interpretation that a researcher makes of an account. That is, it requires that the user go through a particular text and make explicit the logical connections they discern within this. The ensuing analysis is then concerned with whether this logical structure is internally consistent. However, the problem here is that this process in effect requires the researcher to "fix" logical errors within the original data text—the analysis will not work on "faulty" logic, and yet this may be precisely the structure of the original. Thus when using Ethno to look at the structure of Co-Operative Guildwomen's accounts in order to compare the structures of these, it became apparent that in order to make this package "work" the researcher necessarily had to supply "missing" logical information (by best-guessing what this might be) and to exclude or re-work aspects of the account which could not be connected even by such means.

Thus far we have discussed some problematic features of these packages without making explicit the evaluative criteria we are using in order to pinpoint such problems. We now move on to discuss the evaluative criteria that UCAQD developed to evaluate the software under consideration, particularly discussing aspects of the conceptual and epistemological heritage upon which our evaluation draws.

CONTRA VARIABLE ANALYSIS

The criteria used to evaluate the different software packages were importantly influenced by Blumer's (1956) critique of variable analysis. Blumer begins his critique by considering how variables are selected, in the sense of asking what criteria are used to select-in some and select-out others. Usually this is treated as completely taken for granted; however, as Blumer points out, it is so pivotal to the ensuing analysis and indeed the analytic outcomes that it should command detailed attention at the outset of research. Relatedly, he suggests that the researcher should consider whether the selected variables are generic or substantive in character, and proposes that the selection of the generic (the usual choice) is one which leads the researcher to ignore the importance of contextual meanings: the "here and now" of the interactional context within which the research was carried out and which provides the setting for the meanings which research subjects invest in their responses.

For Blumer this concentration on the generic leads the researcher to ignore the "test of interpretive understanding." That is, the contextual interpretations and meanings assigned to a concept, such as "class" or "ethnicity" or "gender," may be very different from those assigned theoretically and generically. Thus, any attempt to understand interaction needs to attend to the substantive and contextual, rather than assume a synonymity between the substantive and the generic which actually gives analytic primacy to the generic.

Built into variable analysis is a related assumption, that if variables can be correlated, then this means that the link between them is causal, with one variable (the independent variable) causally affecting the other (the dependent variable). However, Blumer insists that correlation between variables says nothing about causality (an argument of course shared by most philosophers of the social sciences and of history), but also, and perhaps more unusually, he also insists that to the extent to which causality exists it lies within the interpretive connections which inform social action. For Blumer, then, causality is not a researcher's discovery but rather an a priori feature of social life which is discernible only by focusing analytically upon the contextual specifics of social interaction.

Relatedly, Blumer criticizes the way that variables are construed as "clean-cut" and mutually-exclusive. Looked at substantively and contextually, such variables are never present like this, as obviously and incontrovertibly *the* feature(s) of the particular aspect of social life under scrutiny. Not only may different researchers with different analytic projects in mind "see" different things within the data, but also the saliences of these may be entirely different for the social actors involved.

Here Blumer forces us back to the most fundamental point of all: are we concerned with "their" understandings or "ours"? Interestingly, however, Blumer is not interested in researchers developing better means of interpreting and analyzing "their" understandings, but instead in encouraging researchers both to recognize that "their" and "our" concepts are not synonymous, and to develop a sharper and more critical awareness of the specificities of "ours."

It will be obvious that Blumer has few if any sympathies with the conventional variable analysis approach. Moreover, it is clear that he sees this approach as not only characterizing quantitative and positivist research, but also much qualitative analysis as well. What we draw from Blumer's still highly pertinent discussion is that researchers need to commence any piece of research by asking some fundamental and linked questions about just what kind of analysis they want to carry out and what kinds of analytic outcomes they want the research to produce.

Having thought about the points that Blumer raises, we concluded that there were three basic issues we wanted to explore when evaluating the dedicated qualitative software packages introduced earlier. The first of these issues is what the *analytic purposes* of using such a package are; the second is what *analytic outcomes* are desired; and the third concerns what *epistemological/methodological options* are affected by the way the various packages structure the kind of analysis that can be carried out.

The first issue is whether the data are being analyzed to make explicit—indeed, to "discover"—ideas which are seen as somehow a priori embedded within the data, or whether the data are being analyzed to explore theoretical ideas derived from outside of the data, from the debates and concerns of the wider discipline or a subset within it. That is, the fundamental issue here is *whose concepts* are seen as the focus of analysis, and therefore whether the analyst is to be seen as merely a technician working within the parameters of a grounded theory approach, or, in contrast, whether instead the researcher's own conceptual structure is seen as the analytic focus.

This issue can be seen particularly clearly by comparing the fundamental precepts upon which The Ethnograph and NUD•IST are based. The clearly stated purpose of The Ethnograph is to act as an aid to formulating and articulating the researcher's own concepts and interpretations. Thus, the manual states "we *add* our own record of reflection as we talk about their talk—and thus we do our own code mapping within the etic realm of our own particular interests" (The Ethnograph Manual, p. 4), with this "etic realm" of the researcher's interpretations and "mappings" being contrasted with the "emic realm" of the subjects' record of action and talk. However, in comparison NUD•IST is positioned within a particular version of "grounded theory" as a means of pinpointing a conceptual structure perceived as "in" the data, pre-existent and independent of the researcher's constructions of it. In effect NUD•IST is positioned as a means of "discovery" of social phenomena independent of theoretical or any other kind of preconception on the part of the researcher, seeing theory as something which "emerges" from the data itself Thus, the manual says "A significant feature of most qualitative analysis methodologies is the requirement to let one's theories about the data emerge from the data in an on-going cycle until a stable overall theoretical picture has been obtained" (Reference Manual p.72).

Interestingly, however, the same issue is dealt with in a very different way from both of these packages by Info Select. Its "neuron search," sometimes characterized as the "John Wayne factor," is seen to mimic or simulate the way the human mind draws connections between apparently unconnected elements—guns, cowboys, and "Duke"—to reach a conclusion different in kind from the constitutive elements—John Wayne. However, while this is, implicitly at least, a simulation of the "neuron search" of the researcher, it carries out this search on elements within the data. Thus, rather than adopting a position on either side of a divide between "researcher's constructions" and "subjects' constructions," Info Select instead occupies a middle ground.

The second issue is concerned with the analytic outcomes which are desired. Here it needs to be decided whether the intention is to produce what is in effect a variable analysis of the qualitative data under consideration, or whether the desired outcome is to make apparent the constructed interpretation of the data by the researcher/analyst. That is, a "variable analysis" approach is one which progressively works the data in order to construct a set of concepts linked together to form variables, in what is an exercise largely similar to constructing variables in quantitative forms of analysis. The alternative here is instead for the constructed interpretation of the data by the researcher/analyst to be the desired outcome of the research process, a radically different approach and one consonant with Blumer's critique of variable analysis.

We have already noted that NUD•IST encourages the researcher to produce hierarchically related conceptual trees; however, once this is realized, it is in fact possible to work in a different way, by indexing only on one level and not relating these "levels" or nodes in the suggested way. Thus while the structure of NUD•IST encourages a researcher to work in a "variable analysis" frame, this is by no means determined by the package, which can be used in a way that is more consonant with the approach to qualitative analysis so powerfully enunciated by Blumer. However, as a package intended specifically for the analysis of how the researcher interprets the structure of an account, paradoxically Ethno requires the researcher to re-work elements of this account whenever its structure is positioned by the workings of the software as "logically faulty," an interesting and highly consequential contradiction in its operation. The more general point we are making here is that neither package is so tightly tied to the particular epistemological position presented as the beginning user might suppose.

Another illustration of this concerns the contradiction between NUD•IST, positioned within grounded theorizing, and its links to a firmly foundationalist and quantified approach; two elements of this package in particular produce this effect. One is the way it presents an initial decision which has to be made concerning what kind of "text unit" the data will be broken down into in order to produce counts of these; the other, relatedly, is the selling point of its ability to be linked with SPSS and thus to produce more sophisticated joint statistical analysis of quantified elements of the qualitative data. Both the choice of text unit and the move to quantification are presented without consideration of the conditions under which the data has been produced and whether the choices made are epistemologically appropriate. We are by no means suggesting that qualitative data should never be "quantified"; rather that this is a methodological and epistemological issue and not merely a technical one.

This particular contradiction between a formal qualitative approach coupled with built-in foundationalist precepts is by no means confined to NUD•IST, for a number of packages additional to those evaluated by UCAQD, such as Aquad and Hyper Research (a MacIntosh package), are intended for hypothesis building and testing. Theirs is clearly a very different approach than, for example, the objections to a quantified approach to qualitative analysis that underpins The Ethnograph, for even when its manual notes the ability to produce counts it also cautions the user to consider the epistemological ramifications of doing so.

The third issue is concerned with epistemological and methodological options and the ways in which each of the software packages, by structuring the data analysis, also structure epistemological possibilities. One key example here concerns whether the software is presented in a way which encourages all cases (that is, all the data relating to particular individuals who are included as subjects within the research) to be treated as part of *one single data set*, or whether *individual cases* can be preserved and analyzed as precisely individual cases.

As we have already noted, NUD•IST can be "subverted" so that a variable tree structure is not produced, by working the data though indexing nodes which are not then hierarchically connected. In addition to this, each case within a larger data set can be entered as separate nodes in their own right. Thus, all cases can be entered in NUD•IST as separate nodes; the analysis then proceeds by indexing concepts (which can be applied to all cases or only some) which can themselves be stored as separate nodes. Although somewhat complicated to describe, the actual procedures, once these are known about, can be put into operation fairly easily. However, no such procedures have to be carried out to enable an exactly similar approach within askSam. Here each case is simply entered as a separate file, and the package can move across large numbers of separate files extremely quickly and easily by using a "keywords" approach to building concepts or by using its hypertext facility.

These issues indicate the extent to which these packages are analytically and epistemologically open or closed—or rather the extent to which they may be both open and closed regarding different features. Our concern with epistemological openness derives from the fact that what are apparently non-epistemological considerations—how cases are data entered, how and if variables are constructed and so forth—actually close down or limit the epistemological possibilities. We go on to discuss this in more detail.

EPISTEMOLOGICAL OPENNESS

Here this for us central notion of "epistemological openness" is used to examine a number of what are apparently merely technical features of the various packages evaluated, but which have what are actually important conceptual and epistemological consequentialities which researchers need to be aware of and take on board should they decide to use them. That is, there is nothing inherently "wrong" with any of these features so long as researchers are aware both of their existence and of their analytic ramifications, and knowingly accept these or find ways of subverting them.

We begin by interpreting the notion of "openness" as the extent to which a particular package imposes a pre-structure on the data at the stages of either data entry or data classification. In this respect, neither askSam nor Info Select (nor Word for Windows, discussed later) pre-structure the data at all. That is, analysis within both of these packages is carried out on "raw data" by the use of keywords and wild cards which can be decided and changed almost immediately, and not through a more permanent and less easily removed system of tagging and classifying passages. The Ethnograph is a half-way house in this regard, for while its analytic procedures necessarily involve tagging and classifying, nevertheless there is no need to organize the tagged passages in a hierarchy which forms what is in effect a variable tree. This is unlike NUD•IST, which encourages researchers to produce hierarchies of variables. While the construction of such hierarchies within NUD•IST can be subverted by researchers determined to avoid its analytic constraints, nonetheless users would have to be sufficiently knowledgeable about the consequences of following the type of analysis encouraged to resist this. Ethno is entirely concerned with the analyst's interpretation of the logical *structure* of the data within a case, not its *content* as such, and it proceeds by constraining the analyst to specify their interpretation of these logical connections. This results in an abstract notion of "logic" being imposed over the data itself for in order to make the software "work," the researcher has to specify such connections including by supplying absent ones and repairing "faulty" ones. Apparently entirely "open" with regard to the original data itself in practice Ethno requires as a condition of its operation analytic closures over this data.

Even something as apparently trivially technical as the very specific requirements concerning line length at the data entry stage of The Ethnograph and NUD•IST may operate analytic closures. For example, this may occur if the researcher is concerned with conversational or generally structural aspects of how people present their accounts. Thus, the overlaps between one person speaking very quickly and saying a good deal, and another sighing or uttering one emphatic word, may be the crucial topic of investigation, but The Ethnograph's 40 character and NUD•IST's 69 character maximum line limits can prevent its representation within the ensuing layout of the data. Similar epistemological consequentiality derives from the way that NUD•IST requires the researcher, prior to data entry, to decide whether the "text unit" of analysis is a line, sentence, or paragraph. Such a choice cannot be avoided, for the package itself will otherwise impose its own "decision" wherever there is a carriage return in the text data. This apparently insignificant choice influences the workings of the package thereafter, for the text unit is the basis of the counts and statistics that the package produces. In itself this is not a problem—after all, the researcher can choose to stop their analysis short of producing counts—but if counts are produced then what remains a problem is that the "text unit" can contain internally highly variable units. Lines are perhaps the least contentious text unit, for all lines in NUD•IST are a maximum of 69 characters, but sentences can be of radically different lengths, as can paragraphs. Thus the counts produced here are likely not to be of comparable entities: "two sentences" can include one of 300 lines and one of one word only, and "two paragraphs" can contain one of many sentences of highly variable length and one of a single word or sentence.

Another way the epistemological possibilities can be affected by "technicalities" is through choice of what constitutes the unit of analysis, individual cases (as with our Mass-Observation project), or all cases grouped together (as with the Co-Operative Guild project). Thus NUD•IST proceeds on the basis that a researcher will want to carry out an integral analysis across all cases (this is what it terms a "project"), whereas The Ethnograph starts with the assumption that the researcher will be concerned with individual cases.[8] Again, at the outset this choice may not appear very consequential, although in fact it has profound influences on the kind of analysis that is carried out. Thus a "project" approach would have removed from existence the very features of the Mass-Observation day-diaries we were concerned with analyzing, whereas a "case" approach would have adversely affected our analytic approach to the Guild data.

We have already noted various problems with the variable approach to analyzing qualitative data sets. A further aspect of this is the often implicit related assumption that such "variables" are causally connected, as demonstrated by their "tree-like" relationship, and that the researcher should be concerned with establishing the direction and even strength of causality. Thus, although it never uses the term causality, nonetheless Ethno uses the formal apparatus of prior necessary conditions ("prerequisites") and antecedent outcomes that constitute a causal analysis. By requiring the researcher to specify prerequisites, the researcher is in fact being required to make judgments as to causal patterns and relationships. In this connection, the notion of a "variable tree" can also be seen to assume causal patterns and connection between lower and higher elements within the variable structure, for its tree structure in itself assigns meaning to the position of any element within the tree. The packages that encourage the researcher to "nest" concepts and to construct variables within variable trees, so in effect build into the ensuing analysis a causal approach that is actually at odds with how we at least understand the precepts of a qualitative standpoint within the social sciences.

The analysis carried out on our two data sets, and the consequent evaluation of the software packages used, suggests that each has both strengths and weaknesses when evaluated "empty"; However, when evaluated "full" and in relation to the range of issues discussed above, a rather different evaluative outcome results. The packages that most pre-structure the data are certainly the most sophisticated in terms of the array of techniques made available to the researcher. However, at the same time these are also the packages that most constrain researchers to analyze *qualitative* data as though it is actually *quantitative* data, by producing a form of hierarchically organized variable analysis and assigning significance in quantitative terms—the very approach that Blumer's discussion is intended to counsel qualitative researchers against.

USING A WORD PROCESSING PACKAGE AS AN ANALYTIC AID

At this point we want to suspend the assumption that a dedicated qualitative analysis package should be used, and instead consider the analytic facilities that a good word processing package can provide a qualitative researcher. We do so by considering three linked points: first, if the basic aim in using a dedicated package is to provide efficient means of "clerical assistance and data management" to the researcher, then how does a word processing package measure up against the dedicated packages; second, to what extent can a word processing package provide facilities in addition to these basic clerical and management ones; and, third, what factors can usefully be taken into account when deciding whether to use a word processing package or a dedicated package.

The kinds of factors useful to take into account here importantly include the fact that it is necessary to use a word processing package anyway, even if one then also uses a dedicated package. A word processing package must be used, first to set up the data in a form to enable it to be entered into such a package, and, second, to later write-up the results of analysis. There are obvious advantages if the same package could also be used to analyze the data. Not only would a great deal of time "cleaning up the data" be saved, so too would time spent in learning how to use another package, transferring data between word processing files and dedicated package files and then back again.

Having used a variety of other pre-Windows and Windows word processing packages, we concluded that Word for Windows provided the best facilities, including its ease of use (aided by an excellent on-line tutorial and good back-up services provided by Microsoft), its speed, the variety and sophistication of the facilities it provides, and also, as a Windows package, the ability to link different kinds of material—textual, numerical, graphical, and oral. Moreover, Word for Windows provides equally excellent facilities for the perhaps humbler but crucially necessary clerical and management tasks involved in qualitative data analysis, including formatting, cutting and pasting, and moving (including moving data) between different files. In addition, Word for Windows contains some extremely sophisticated features for analyzing text-based data, including the capacity to produce indices, counts of words or phrases, and tables and graphs, "hidden" marking and annotation facilities and more. Moreover, its macro facility enables it to be programmed to aid more complex textual analysis, including line numbering both on-screen text and hard copies of the original data.

We used Word for Windows to help analyze our qualitative data sets. As using a word processing passage in this way is still fairly unusual, it may be helpful to describe the various steps involved in this.

1. Clean up the original text and format as required—and of course all of the original emphases can stay, as the text will be worked as a word processing rather than a text file.[9]
2. Set the appropriate line and page margins; these can be changed at will and very speedily.
3. Run a macro to line number the text both on screen and on hard copy.[10]
4. First save and then print out a line numbered reference hard copy of the original data text. Keep one copy of this on hard disk and a back-up on a floppy disk, neither of which should be used other than for archiving/backup purposes.
5. Create a working copy of the original data file by saving it with a different name from the original; preferably keep all the worked analysis on a floppy disk (avoid hard disk crashes, the researcher's nightmare) and at the end of every day create a backup copy of this on another floppy disk.
6. Photocopy the line numbered reference copy at least once, preferably more. File at least one copy, and keep one as the working copy.
7. Read the reference hard copy many times in order to decide on an analytic framework (provisional and revisable) around which it can be analyzed.
8. Work manually on a working hard copy to mark up words, phrases, and so forth and to attach index names to these on the hard copy itself. Refer back to the analytic framework while doing so and revise in the light of experience in working the data set.
9. Type into the hard disk copy of the original reference file the field names of this indexing and create a page numbered index of the data (one level, using just the index facility, or two levels using the contents facility as well).
10. Use the annotation facility to write notes attached to the data text explaining your interpretation of what each field name means; otherwise this can be easily forgotten.
11. Print out the page numbered index and create a separate word processing file in which the index is saved; changes to this can then be made to this now ordinary word processing file without affecting the original data text/index itself.

12. Working from the marked up hard copy of the data text and the print out of the page numbered text, attach line numbers to each of the index codes, initially by writing these on the print out and then typing them onto the word processed index file.
13. Print out a finalized word processed index file, and then use this to create an outline of the analytic account of the research.
14. Write an outline of the report/paper/chapter and save in an appropriately labeled file. Have open at the same time the working copy of the original data text. Go back and forth between the two using the "Window" pull-down menu.
15. Use "copy" and "paste" from the main screen toolbar in order to copy into your outline relevant passages, quotations, and so forth.
16. Write up the report, paper, chapter, thesis, around this.

Of course Word for Windows also has analytic limitations. The principal such limitation we have found is that while it can be used to aid the analysis of very large amounts of data, and while very large numbers of individual files can be stored and analyzed, it is not possible to analyze *across* different files other than by doing so manually. That is, it is not possible to set up an aspect of analysis (say, using the indexing facility) and then run it automatically on a number of files; this instead has to be produced by bringing each file on screen and then doing it manually. The alternative strategy of placing all files as cases within a single "project file" makes it extremely difficult to preserve each case separate from all others: line-numbering of each case, for example, then has to be done manually. Still, it is important to keep in mind that *all* these packages have limitations of one kind or another, including the necessity to carry out much of the work by marking up manually onto successive hard copies, and that for research where preserving individual cases is unimportant this particular "limitation" will not be experienced as such. What is important we think is that researchers should be aware of such limitations *in relation to the specificities of particular data sets*, find means of subverting them where possible, and then either working round them or else going elsewhere.

In "answer" to the three points outlined at the start of this section, then, first, Word for Windows is greatly superior to any of the dedicated packages regarding the fundamentally necessary clerical assistant and data management tasks. Second, it provides an excellent range of more advanced facilities which are very useful indeed for a qualitative researcher and which may make use of a dedicated package redundant, depending on the particular research at hand. We discuss the third point, choosing between a good word processing package and a dedicated package, in our conclusion.

CONCLUSION

Having used both Word for Windows and the five dedicated packages, our conclusion is that qualitative researchers should consider using a good word processing package as their basic analytic aid, and that only if they want to do something that this package cannot do should they then consider using a dedicated package. That is, for many researchers, the facilities provided in a good word processing package will be sufficient to the analysis required, or, if not, the researcher would be best advised to use a dedicated package for specific research tasks. The seduction of the dedicated packages is that because they have capacities, these are then used to the limits possible. A result can be the over-expenditure of time and the over-analysis of data relative both to its importance and to the written product which will result: a not very interesting data set relentlessly analyzed over a year or more, which then after more time spent "writing up" results in a small part of a doctoral thesis or aspects of a couple of working papers or journal articles.

The particular research tasks that we think the packages we have discussed are particularly useful for are as follows. The Ethnograph and NUD•IST are particularly good at retrieving and placing in a separate file a range of pieces of text which have been coded or indexed in a particular way, complete with the line-numbers of this text. This can be done manually using Word for Windows of course, but its mechanized extremely speedy production here makes these two packages very attractive in this regard. In carrying out such initial searches for particular kinds of textual data, NUD•IST's wildcard facility is an additional bonus here, greatly facilitating searching and finding. Whether the time-savings made through using these facilities will outweigh time-expenditure in learning how to use them and preparing text for data entry within them will depend on a number of factors, and particularly the size of the total data set. The larger the data set, the greater the likelihood that time-savings will exceed time-expenditures.

The program askSam is a package that we associate with its great speed and flexibility in carrying out searches across large amounts of data and large numbers of files; and its Hypertext facility—escribed inadequately in a few lines buried in an appendix—provides a particularly flexible aid to a researcher getting to know their data set. It is all the more disappointing that even the latest version of this underrated package does not permit line numbering of text, for with this facility askSam would in our view be a key aid for all qualitative researchers.

Ethno constrains the researcher to think about the structure of research accounts, something that no other of these packages does, and while content is obviously important, so too is the structure of accounts, *how* people say and write what they do. Moreover, for those researchers interested in formulating a causal-type analysis, Ethno provides an interesting means of doing so although it is perhaps the hardest of these packages to learn to use.

Info Select has undoubted strengths as a package intended for business users. However, its neuron search does not live up to expectation and in our view it is a non-runner for a research use.

Throughout this paper we have stressed the importance of thinking through exactly what kind of characteristics a particular qualitative data set has, and what style of analysis and what analytic outcomes a researcher is after. The existence of dedicated software packages to aid the analysis of qualitative data does not foreclose the necessity of doing so, indeed their existence makes doing so even more important. Such packages are best seen, as we have termed it throughout, as "analytic *aids*," not something which in their own right analyzes. We have also argued that *all* such packages produce epistemological effects and that this in itself is no bad thing, so long as researchers are aware of it and choose software aids that do not undermine or vitiate their particular epistemological stance. We do not accept a "variable analysis" approach that works with qualitative data in the same way as quantitative data. However, it is certainly not necessary to share this view to be interested in treating such software as a suitable topic for sociological analysis in its own right, nor to be concerned about the lack of open debate concerning the epistemological consequentiality of using such software.

NOTES

1. A good many more than these five are available, most of which have been written by researchers for particular purposes and then distributed more widely. We evaluated packages which are available on a commercial or semi-commercial basis. The marketing of such packages is interesting in its own right, although we do not discuss it here.

2. It resulted from a joint bid between the departments of sociology, social policy, and anthropology involving Liz Stanley, Duncan Scott, and David Rheubottom, with the project's research fellow being Bogusia Temple.

3. This research was carried out as part of the Rochdale project within the Social Change and Economic Life Initiative which was based at the University of Manchester. The Manchester Rochdale SCEL project was funded by the ESRC under grant No. G13250017; we are grateful to the ESRC for its support.

4. There were also ethnographic field notes written by one of the researchers (Stanley) involved in this research; however, these were excluded from "the data set" utilized by UCAQD because they were handwritten and transcription specifically for UCAQD was not possible within its funding limits.

5. This was carried out as unfunded development research to underpin two, unsuccessful, bids made to the ESRC. Publications so far from the research include Stanley (1990, 1992, 1993, 1994, 1995).

6. The National Panel was first constituted during the original 1937-1949 phase of Mass-Observation. Staff of the Mass-Observation Archive at the University of Sussex have reconstituted aspects of the National Panel's activities, to explore the conditions of life in 1980s and 1990s Britain; see here Sheridan (1993a, 1993b).

7. NUDIST is an acronym standing for "Non-numerical Unstructured Data Indexing, Searching and Theorising."

8. In fact it is possible to work in both ways within both packages, but nonetheless they start from very different assumptions and it is these that are likely to influence how anyone not already familiar with these packages will use them.

9. When transferring data into one of the dedicated packages, this is done in text format. Text format or ASCII removes all formatting apart from carriage-returns, and so underlining or italics or other formatting means of indicating emphases cannot be used within the dedicated packages.

10. With the help of Microsoft's technical support staff we have written a macro to line number on screen as well as on hard copy (Word for Windows can do the latter although not the former without this macro). Copies of the macro on 3 and 1/2" disks are available free from us, by sending a check for £5 to cover the cost of the disk, postage, and package to Liz Stanley. A condition of its supply is that full acknowledgment should be given in any written work which makes use of this macro; a form of words for doing so will be supplied with the disk.

REFERENCES

Blumer, H.
1956 "Sociological Analysis and the 'Variable.'" *American Sociological Review* 21: 683-690

Dey, I.
1993 *Qualitative Data Analysis: A User-Friendly Guide for Social Scientists.* London: Routledge.

Fielding, N., and R. Lee (Eds).
1992 *Using Computers in Qualitative Research.* London: Sage Publications.

Griffin, L.
1993 "Narrative, Event-structure Analysis and Causal Interpretation in Historical Sociology." *American Journal of Sociology* 98: 1094-1133.

Heise, D.
1992 "Event-structure Analysis: A Qualitative Model of Quantitative Research." Pp. 136-163 in *Using Computers in Qualitative Research*, edited by N. Fielding and R. Lee. London: Sage Publications.

Richards, L., and T. Richards.
1992 "The Transformation of Qualitative Method: Computational Paradigms and Research Processes." Pp.38-53 in *Using Computers in Qualitative Research*, edited by N. Fielding and R. Lee. London: Sage Publications.

Seidal, J.
1992 "Method and Madness in the Application of Computer Technology to Qualitative Data Analysis." Pp. 107-116 in *Using Computers in*

Qualitative Research, edited by N. Fielding and R. Lee. London: Sage Publications.

Sheridan, D.
1993a "Writing to the Archive: Mass-Observation as Autobiography." *Sociology* 27: 27-40.

Sheridan, D.
1993b "Ordinary Hardworking Folk: Volunteer Writers in Mass-Observation, 1937-50 and 1981-91." *Feminist Praxis* 37/38: 1-34.

Stanley, L.
1990 "The Archaeology of a Mass-Observation Project." Manchester University Occasional Papers in Sociology, No. 27.

Stanley, L.
1992 "The Economics of Everyday Life: A Mass-Observation Project in Bolton." *North-West Labour History* 17: 95-102.

Stanley, L.
1993 "Issues in Reading the Mass-Observation Day-diaries." *Feminist Praxis* 37/38: 81-92.

Stanley, L.
1994 "Women Have Servants and Men Never Eat: Issues in Reading 'Gender' in Mass-Observation's 1937 Day-diaries." *Women's History Review* 3: 2.

Stanley, L.
1995 *Sex Survey, 1949-1994*. London: Taylor & Francis.

NOTES ON CONTRIBUTORS

Derrick Armstrong is a lecturer in the Division of Education, University of Sheffield, Sheffield, England.

Paul Atkinson is a professor of sociology in the School of Social and Administrative Studies, University of Wales, College of Cardiff, Wales.

Robert G. Burgess is a professor of sociology and director of the Centre for Educational Development, Appraisal and Research (CEDAR), University of Warwick, Coventry, England.

Nigel G. Fielding is a reader in sociology at the University of Surrey, Guildford, England.

Sharlene Hesse-Biber is an associate professor and chair in the Department of Sociology, Boston College.

Emma Lakin ia a final-year student at the University of Central England in Birmingham, England.

Raymond M. Lee is a reader in social research in the Department of Social Policy and Social Science, Royal Holloway College, University of London, Egham, England.

Wilma Mangabeira is a lecturer and research fellow at the Centre for Research into Innovation, Culture and Technology, Brunel University, England.

Christopher J. Pole is a lecturer in the Department of Sociology and the Centre for Educational Development, Appraisal and Research (CEDAR) at the University of Warwick, Coventry, England.

Lyn Richards is an associate professor and reader in sociology at La Trobe University, Melbourne, Australia.

Annemarie Sprokkereef is a research fellow at the University of Essex, Colchester, England.

Liz Stanley is a reader in sociology at the University of Manchester, England.

Bogusia Temple is a research fellow in the Department of Social Policy and Social Work, University of Manchester, England.

Anna Weaver is a research assistant in the School of Social and Administrative Studies, University of Wales, College of Cardiff, Wales.

AUTHOR INDEX

SUBJECT INDEX